Real-Life MDA

Morgan Kaufmann OMG Press

Morgan Kaufmann Publishers and the Object Management Group™ (OMG) have joined forces to publish a line of books addressing business and technical topics related to OMG's large suite of software standards.

OMG is an international, open membership, not-for-profit computer industry consortium that was founded in 1989. The OMG creates standards for software used in government and corporate environments to enable interoperability and to forge common development environments that encourage the adoption and evolution of new technology. OMG members and its board of directors consist of representatives from a majority of the organizations that shape enterprise and Internet computing today.

OMG's modeling standards, including the Unified Modeling Language™ (UML®) and Model Driven Architecture® (MDA), enable powerful visual design, execution and maintenance of software, and other processes—for example, IT Systems Modeling and Business Process Management. The middleware standards and profiles of the Object Management Group are based on the Common Object Request Broker Architecture® (CORBA) and support a wide variety of industries.

More information about OMG can be found at http://www.omg.org/.

Forthcoming Morgan Kaufmann OMG Press Titles

UML 2 Certification Guide: Fundamental and Intermediate Exams
Tim Weilkiens and Bernd Oestereich

Real-Life MDA: Solving Business Problems with Model Driven Architecture
Michael Guttman and John Parodi

Architecture Driven Modernization: A Series of Industry Case Studies
Bill Ulrich

Real-Life MDA

Solving Business Problems with Model Driven Architecture

Michael Guttman
John Parodi

ELSEVIER

AMSTERDAM • BOSTON • HEIDELBERG • LONDON
NEW YORK • OXFORD • PARIS • SAN DIEGO
SAN FRANCISCO • SINGAPORE • SYDNEY • TOKYO
Morgan Kaufmann Publishers is an imprint of Elsevier

MORGAN KAUFMANN PUBLISHERS

658.4038
G98r

Publisher	Denise E. M. Penrose
Senior Editor	Tim Cox
Publishing Services Manager	George Morrison
Production Editor	Dawnmarie Simpson
Assistant Editor	Michelle Ward
Assistant Editor	Mary E. James
Cover Design	Alisa Andreola
Text Design	Chen Design Associates
Composition	Integra Software Services, Pvt., Ltd.
Technical Illustration	Integra Software Services, Pvt., Ltd.
Copyeditor	Graphic World Publishing Services
Proofreader	Graphic World Publishing Services
Indexer	Graphic World Publishing Services
Interior printer	The Maple-Vail Book Manufacturing Group
Cover printer	Phoenix Color, Inc.

Morgan Kaufmann Publishers is an imprint of Elsevier.
500 Sansome Street, Suite 400, San Francisco, CA 94111

This book is printed on acid-free paper.

Library of Congress Cataloging-in-Publication Data
Guttman, Michael.
Real-life MDA: solving business problems with model driven architecture/Michael Guttman and John Parodi.
 p. cm.
 Includes bibliographical references and index.
 ISBN 0-12-370592-4 (alk. paper)
1. Information technology—Management—Case studies.   2. Computer software—Development—Case studies.   3. Software architecture–Case studies.   4. System design—Case studies.   5. Management information systems—Case studies.   I. Parodi, John.   II. Title.
 HD30.2.G884 2005
 658.4′038—dc22
                                                                2006023686

ISBN 13: 978-0-12-370592-1
ISBN 10: 0-12-370592-4

For information on all Morgan Kaufmann publications,
visit our Web site at www.mkp.com or www.books.elsevier.com

Printed in the United States of America
06 07 08 09 10   5 4 3 2 1

To Lynn and Alison

ABOUT THE AUTHORS

Michael Guttman is a information technology industry executive with a impressive 30-year track record delivering innovative solutions and professional services to Global 1000 clients. He is also a well-known visionary in the areas of IT strategic planning and enterprise architecture, and has been active in the development of a number of industry standards, including CORBA, UML, and MDA. Mr. Guttman has also served as Director of the MDA FastStart program for the Object Management Group (OMG), a 500+ member international software industry consortium.

Mr. Guttman is currently CTO of The Voyant Group, responsible for the company's technical vision and strategy, including the development all professional services offerings. Mr. Guttman was formerly CEO of the Miriam Institute, a IT strategy company which recently merged with Voyant. Previously, Mr. Guttman was Director of Strategic Technology at IONA Technologies, PLC and CTO and co-founder of Genesis Development, which was merged into IONA in June of 2000.

Mr. Guttman is the co-author of two other books, "*The Object Technology Revolution*" (1996), and "*Developing E-Business Systems and Architectures*" (2000). He is a regular columnist in Software Magazine and serves as a Senior Consultant on enterprise architecture at the The Cutter Consortium. He lives in Chadds Ford, PA, with his girlfriend Lynn and brother David, where he enjoys hiking, collecting antiques, and playing the piano.

John Parodi has more than twenty-five years of experience in software technical communication, including award-winning white papers, user documentation and trade press articles, on topics that include middleware, enterprise integration, security, software architecture, and development methodologies. He recently acted as editor for the book "*The MDA Journal: Model Driven Architecture Straight From The Masters*" (2004).

During his career, Mr. Parodi has worked in a number of capacities for several leading software vendors and professional services companies, including DEC, IONA, and Genesis Development Corporation. His favorite jobs have involved capturing and articulating the ideas of technical staff.

Mr. Parodi currently works as a consultant and serves as the Director of Technical Communications with The Voyant Group. He lives with his wife Alison, and cat Duster, in central New Hampshire.

CONTENTS

7   INTERACTIVE OBJECTS/DAIMLER CASE STUDY: AUTOMOTIVE INDUSTRY   137

8   SUMMING UP THE PARTS   155

FOREWORD

In a single generation the IT industry has successfully automated many of the most common and mundane information processing tasks of the modern enterprise. This has allowed organizations of all kinds—and the people they employ—to scale up their operational scope and efficiency beyond the wildest dreams of pre-IT yesteryear.

But precisely because this kind of basic scalability is now largely taken for granted, the computing industry finds itself at a crossroads. Some industry experts, most notably Harvard's Nicholas Carr, have even asserted that this commoditization of traditional IT begs the question of whether IT even matters anymore[1]. Therefore, many businesses are now working diligently to restructure and downsize their traditional IT functions, primarily through such vehicles as acquiring third-party packages, outsourcing and out-servicing.

Many of these new IT restructuring approaches certainly make some immediate economic sense. (In fact, as you will see, some of the case studies presented in this book actually address them directly.) But does that mean that IT really doesn't matter at all anymore?

This book clearly demonstrates otherwise. In six potent case studies, the authors have captured the dynamics of a new breed of IT organizations that are using a powerful approach, MDA, in order to shed their traditional role of 'data janitors' and refocus on the task of directly helping the businesses they serve become significantly more agile, innovative and competitive.

What makes MDA so powerful in this respect? What is leading these and many other organizations to explore, adopt, and adapt MDA to become more agile and competitive? MDA is powerful because it synergistically exploits three proven

---

1   Does IT Matter? Information Technology and the Corrosion of Competitive Advantage, Harvard Business School Press. Carr, Nicholas. 2004.

principles of industrial production: models (or blueprints), componentization, and patterns. We cannot mindlessly apply these principles in the same way that we apply them to the production of physical things, but there are many useful lessons to draw from industrial experience.

Even when they are not explicitly labeled as such, you can readily see how each of those industrial principles is applied in every case study in this book. In each case, MDA was used to create formal models of the desired solution using customized tooling that enforces precise design and architectural patterns. The resulting models then went through a series of formalized MDA transformations that ultimately produced deployable software artifacts assembled from standardized, reusable, architecturally-compliant components.

Now, there are certainly other books that more thoroughly describe the theory and mechanics of MDA, but this book chooses to demonstrate the *use* of MDA from a different and perhaps more visceral and human viewpoint. In this book, what you will see are six different sets of real IT practitioners working on six different kinds of mission-critical applications—each figuring out what makes MDA tick, and puzzling out how to best to adapt and apply it to their own unique situations.

It can be (and has been) sensibly argued that, in systematically applying principles of industrial production to the software production lifecycle, MDA represents a 'revolutionary' approach for IT. However, as with other 'revolutionary' approaches to IT, we can confidently predict that the overall industry adoption of MDA will be evolutionary. That is, we can expect MDA tools, standards, and best practices to continuously evolve over the next 10—15 years before MDA, too, ultimately comes to be perceived as a 'commodity.'

Because we are relatively early in this process, the industry needs to have an ongoing conversation about which techniques, tools, and approaches are working, which are not, and why. In this way we can build on that knowledge to move along the transition curve as efficiently as possible. That is another reason why this book is so important—it puts the experiences gained in real-life MDA projects out there for the world to see, in the words of the participants, enriching that conversation.

We also need case studies that more closely examine the organizational impacts of MDA, as these will surely influence the industry transition as much—if not more—than any technical aspects. Once again, this book makes a major contribution, since each of its case study narratives specifically address a wide range of organizational and process issues that are often overlooked in the more common technology-focused books and articles about MDA. As you read through these case studies, it becomes increasingly clear how new roles are emerging (such as Business Modeler, Process Architect, and Services Modeler and Services Architect) that will redefine the way that business and IT must interact in order achieve a new and more effective end-to-end solution creation process.

In particular, each of the book's six case studies also creates a demonstrable link between MDA and service oriented architecture (SOA). The connecting theme is the idea of capturing business logic in technology-independent business models, and then using some form of SOA to realize the elements of those models in a set of modularized, platform-independent service-oriented software components. The industry will gradually move to a reality in which the business process expert, who sits at the Business-IT intersection on the business side, models a business process, while a process architect, who sits at the intersection on the IT side, configures the steps of the business process to invoke pre-built service components. This is the business process management (BPM) vision of executable business models, which the parallel and intertwined evolution of MDA and SOA will bring about in the coming years.

In the end, this book shows that it is not so much that it is easier to do BPM and SOA with MDA, or MDA with BPM and SOA, but that you need all three to reach the goal of providing executable solutions that directly support the need of the business to constantly innovate. Collectively, these case studies document the problems and successes that we face along the way to the long term goal, as well as the importance of providing real business value today, even before the full vision comes to fruition. This is the essence of making IT relevant to the business in the global 'innovation economy.'

David S. Frankel,
SAP Labs

PREFACE

'Model Driven Architecture' (MDA) was formally introduced by the OMG in 2001 as an umbrella term to cover a wide range of OMG software modeling and architecture specifications. Since then, both the set of MDA specifications and their usage have expanded substantially, and the term 'MDA' (and the more generic term 'model-driven') is now widely recognized around the globe—a clear success story for the OMG, the growing community of MDA practitioners, and (we'd like to think) the IT industry at large.

However, at the same time, this has led some people to complain that the term 'MDA' has become much too broad and is in danger of losing its 'essence'—a common enough side effect of success in the constant churn of buzzwords that has always characterized the IT industry. There is an on-going debate about 'exactly what MDA is' or, as one wag put it, 'will the real MDA please stand up.'

Therefore, during the course of writing this book, we tried to get our subjects to provide their own definition of the 'essence of MDA'. The most concise articulation we encountered (again we quote George Thomas of the GSA) is that MDA is "using software to generate software."

In this light, MDA can be seen as simply the latest step on the long journey that began with the replacement of pure binary machine coding by assembly language, and reached various well-known milestones along the way—higher-level (3GL) languages and compliers, OO programming, and a plethora of computer aided software engineering tools. All of these approaches also used increasingly sophisticated software generating tools to create increasingly sophisticated end-user software.

However, MDA actually goes one step further than any of these earlier approaches. Rather than dictate one specific way of 'using software to generate software', it instead provides a framework for managing and integrating many different ways to rationalize and automate the specification, development, deployment, integration and management of software. Given the nature and number of the problems in that space, it would not be possible for any single technical approach to address them all.

That's why a number of people now make use of the 'software factory' analogy to describe the collection of model-driven approaches that encompass MDA. As in a classical factory, there are many distinct areas of concern, each with its own technical sub-culture and vernacular. Somehow, however, all of these pieces fit together in a common architecture that supports the common goal—manufacturing products.

Within the MDA community, what we now see is different people using model-driven approaches to attack different pieces of a huge puzzle—requirements gathering, business analysis, process modeling, systems design, service definition, systems integration, solutions design, platform code generation, automatic transformations, metadata management, etc., etc. MDA is the glue that ties this all together.

The term MDA can thus be used to describe any one of these approaches, or all of them combined. It should therefore be no surprise that if you read six different books on MDA, you may well get six distinct views of what MDA is and how it can best be applied.

This book raises that ante—it provides six different case studies, each with its own view of how to use MDA, all under one single cover. That is, we have tried to paint a picture of the 'essence of MDA' not by being exclusive or proscriptive, but by being inclusive.

Our methodology for choosing and documenting these case studies was relatively simple, and not particularly 'scientific'. Within the MDA professional services community (specifically the OMG's MDA FastStart Program), we asked for volunteers. Successful participants were line developers, architects and project/program managers who claimed to be using MDA in real mission-critical projects which were near or recently past completion. In each case, we interviewed participants both from the end-user companies, and the professional services firms that had been helping them to learn and apply MDA.

Then, with our trusty digital voice recorder rolling, we asked each set of interviewees a similar set of questions about their project and its use of MDA. In particular, we focused on organizational issues—how the use of MDA impacted how they conducted their project, and what longer-term impacts to their organization would likely result from MDA's wider use in the future. That's because we had noticed that such issues are not typically covered in technical books about MDA, even though we know that many people are quite curious about them.

What emerged was a picture of MDA that was largely congruent to what you can read in other more technically oriented books, but from a much broader set of viewpoints and frames of reference. In putting together the final narratives, rather than distill everything we had heard down into our own pet theory about MDA, we chose to quote our sources as much as possible, and minimize our own verbiage and analysis. While the result is not 'scientific,' it does reflect the real and we hope instructive experiences of the participants, who creatively honed MDA to fit their particular needs.

As authors, we found that there was something very refreshing about this approach. Most of the interviewees were being interviewed about their experiences with MDA for the first time, and many seemed to experience interesting revelations and reach new conclusions even during the course of their interviews. At some points, we felt like those talk hosts who get their subjects to open up in ways that surprise everyone.

More importantly, this underlines the dynamic nature of MDA itself. On the surface, MDA may be a set of specifications 'owned' by the OMG. But the OMG is just a commercial organization responding to the needs of the marketplace. It's how MDA is really applied, adapted and perceived in the field that will determine how it develops over time. MDA is still young and growing, and people like the ones we have interviewed for this book are breathing new life into it every day.

Michael Guttman, Chadds Ford, PA
John Parodi, Epsom, NH

ACKNOWLEDGEMENTS

This book would not have been possible without the help of many people scattered across at least five countries and nine time zones. Our thanks go to our case study end-users who were far-sighted enough to adopt MDA to address a business problem, and then were willing to spend some of their valuable time to share their experiences with us. Of the many surprises we encountered in writing this book, perhaps the most pleasant were the insights and honesty these end-users provided.

When George Thomas of the General Services Administration said his project description was "...*not the kind of happy talk you usually see in a case study but it is reality*" he was speaking for himself, but he might have been speaking for all the end-users who participated. We thank him, as well as Chris Fornecker of GSA; Angelo Serra of the State of Ohio Job and Family Services; Walter Siri of Coopservice; Lorenz Lercher of the Austrian Health Authority; David Almeida and Lewis Pearson of Harris Corporation; and Wolfgang Käfer of DaimlerChrysler TSS.

We are also very grateful to the people in the MDA Qualified Service Provider consulting firms, who helped the end-users build their respective business solutions, and who helped us understand the many innovative ways in which MDA is being applied today. We thank Gary Dykstra and Vasil Hlinka of Compuware; Pierfranco Ferronato of Soluta.net; Barry Maybank and Uta Terlinden of Select Business Solutions; Rob Mitchell and Robert Lario of Inherit, LLC; Ed Harrington and Cory Casanave of Data Access Technologies; and Alberto Perandones, Thomas Maurer, and Christian Jäschke of Interactive Objects Software GmbH.

We also want to thank the many other people in the MDA community who gave us help and encouragement in researching and writing this book. This includes all the OMG staff, most especially Bill Hoffman and Richard Soley, whose leadership of the OMG made both MDA and this OMG Press book series possible. We thank our reviewers, Dragan Djuric, Roland Preiß, Art Sedighi, and Dave Hollander. Special thanks also to our long-time colleagues, who contributed many valuable ideas; they are Jason Matthews, Oliver Sims, Michael Rosen, and David S. Frankel (who was also kind enough to review the book and write the foreword).

This book would certainly not have been possible without the steady love and support of our respective families and friends, who helped us endure the many months of trials and tribulations involved in researching, writing, and editing six case studies and integrating them into a single (hopefully) coherent opus. We appreciate that love and support more than these words can express.

Real-Life MDA

CHAPTER ONE
INTRODUCTION

This is a book of case studies in which each study is an example of how some form of Model Driven Architecture® (MDA®) has been introduced into an organization to help solve a real-life business problem. These organizations include three large corporations (two in Europe and one in the United States) whose yearly revenues range from $450 million to $182 billion (U.S. dollars), as well as three governmental agencies (two in the United States and one in Europe) whose sizes span a similar range.

The respective projects involved are commercially important—in some cases vital—to each of these organizations. Moreover, each organization made a conscious and significant commitment to a new approach to managing their software life cycle both when they first decided to use MDA and as they continued to absorb the many implications of that decision. All of them have plans to expand their use of MDA in the future, sometimes in ways they had not previously considered. MDA, it seems, can be somewhat addictive.

So, what is MDA? At the conceptual level, MDA is a holistic approach to improving the entire information technology (IT) life cycle–specification, architecture, design, development, deployment, maintenance, and integration–based on formal modeling. More specifically, MDA is a framework of technical standards progressively being developed by the members of the Object Management Group (OMG)–an open industry consortium supporting this approach–along with a set of usage guidelines for enabling the application of those standards with appropriate tools and processes.

There are a lot of MDA products, even though MDA "compliance" is as yet undefined

Exactly as intended, the release of MDA by the OMG has spawned a wide variety of commercial products purporting to be "MDA compliant." Exactly what that label means is not clear, in that at the moment neither the OMG nor any other organization has any formal mechanism for testing product compliance with any specific MDA standard. There are also a number of vendors selling products that purport to support a "model-driven approach" without specifically claiming to implement or support MDA per se–that is, as defined by the OMG.

Just as predictably, the increasing availability of MDA-based tools is spawning a host of new books and articles about MDA and related approaches (including by the authors of this book). Most of these focus on explaining the theory of MDA, surveying the various standards, or describing in detail the features of specific MDA-based products or techniques. We welcome these books, even if we don't always agree with all of them, and hope for many more to come.

For this book, however, we decided on a different approach—to produce a book about MDA based solely on real-life case studies. In our experience, a good case study is the best (and easiest) way for most people to begin to determine whether or not any particular approach is likely to work for themselves or their organization. If they come to the conclusion that the approach will work for them, they will more likely be willing to wade into the more formidable technical details. Furthermore, by including a healthy half-dozen of such case studies in a single book (drawn from a wide range of organizations and applications) we hope that nearly every reader will be able to find examples that speak directly to their own needs and experience.

So, rather than plunge into MDA per se we simply present the stories of six very different organizations, each of which used MDA to address its business needs in very different ways. For the most part, we believe these case studies stand on their own and speak for themselves (both individually and collectively) and therefore have not tried to embellish them with additional details. That is, what you will read is pretty much just what we were told by the participants.

The really good news is that you don't need to know much about MDA itself to understand these case studies. Anyone with a general familiarity with typical information technology (IT) issues and jargon will have no trouble identifying with most, if not all, of the individuals and organizations involved. That said, for those who might need it we have included a short MDA primer as an appendix, a bibliography, and a glossary that should fill in any remaining conceptual or buzzword gaps.

Otherwise, our primary purpose in writing this book is to "explain" MDA through real-life examples in order to help you, the reader, consider the business case for adopting MDA in your own organization. In each of our case studies, there is an MDA "champion," someone who sensed early on that MDA could really make a difference and who pushed through its acceptance by the organization (at least for the project in question). Perhaps you already are, or will soon be, that person in your own organization.

As you will see in the case studies, that champion may come from IT or from the business itself. He or she may be a C-level corporate officer, an enterprise architect, or a program/project manager. But in every case that champion found a way to demonstrate effectively how the introduction of MDA could substantially benefit the business. Nobody described in the book was just trying to add another

Champions tout MDA's business benefits rather than its shiny new technology

acronym to his or her resume, or merely playing around with some sexy new tools.

That is important to point out, because some people still believe that MDA is just another technical approach for generating code–a new form of CASE (computer-assisted software engineering) based on the popular Unified Modeling Language (UML)–and therefore something far from the concerns of the business. It is true that MDA was originally based on UML, and also true that it is often used to automatically generate code and other software life cycle artifacts. To that extent, MDA carries forward some of the ideas of CASE. But that's really yesterday's news.

MDA is about gaining control over the life cycle of business solutions

Today, as our case studies clearly show, MDA is being applied as an overall approach to gaining control over and systematically improving the entire life cycle of IT solutions–from modeling the overall business and capturing specific solutions requirements to developing, deploying, integrating, and managing many kinds of software components. Today's MDA is less about generating code per se and much more about precisely capturing requirements, enforcing architectural standards, maintaining traceability, and facilitating effective communication between the business and IT (and between different parts of IT).

On the surface, MDA often seems to be different things to different people. To some, MDA is still mainly about generating code from models. To others, MDA is about capturing business requirements more precisely and completely. To yet others, MDA is a way of managing the evolution and integration of existing systems. And as in the story of the blind men and the elephant, all of these perceptions–and more–are equally valid and equally incomplete. This suggests that like the proverbial elephant MDA is already emerging to be much more than the sum of its currently perceived parts.

There, we said it: MDA is a paradigm shift

We really believe that the emergence of MDA represents one of those so-called paradigm shifts, and that it will eventually change everything about the way software systems are specified and built. This is always a controversial position, particularly in IT, which has seen so many supposedly revolutionary "paradigm shifts" come and go. If the readers of this book ultimately reach the same conclusion, it will be because of what they learn from our case studies rather than our attempts to convince them with theory or technical details.

That said, before jumping into the case studies we would like to put our own view about MDA in some type of perspective by way of an analogy. Reasoning by analogy is always risky, but it can sometimes be useful where the very concepts under discussion may be new or unfamiliar to the reader.

By now, most of you have probably already heard the term *software factory*. It may even be that this beguiling label has led some of you to MDA, and even to this very book. The term itself evokes the powerful image of developing software as a form of "manufacturing."

In this context, the "big idea" is that like a modern physical factory the workings of a typical IT department may ultimately be reduced to a set of precisely defined processes supported by appropriate tooling, which can reliably produce high-quality software at ever-decreasing costs and time-to-market. Now, who could argue with that?

Let's remember that the roots of the word *manufacture* are the Latin words for "hand" (*manus*) and "make" (*facere*). Most modern manufacturing industries began as "crafts," in which the production of each unit of a given product was largely a unique one-at-a-time process. The "factory" was just a convenient locale where this took place, not a carefully constructed enabler of the manufacturing process itself.

In the twenty-first century, we rightfully tend to think of the craft-based model of physical production as slow and inefficient, suitable only when some form of artistic output is desired. Moreover, even more serious drawbacks manifest themselves later in a product's life cycle, when it is time to repair or replace a handcrafted unit or to integrate it with other units.

For this reason, the concept of a factory based on an "assembly line" (assembling standardized parts) was invented, ultimately replacing the craft model in nearly all forms of "manufacturing." The current popular definition of manufacturing now almost completely belies its Latin etymology. Few today would expect, or even want, most "manufactured" goods to be literally "handmade."

The notion of assembling finished products from standardized parts is often attributed to the American Eli Whitney (also of cotton gin fame). Whitney famously demonstrated the idea to the U.S. Congress in the late 1790s as a more efficient way of both manufacturing guns and maintaining them in the field. Of course, the basic idea of standardization is much older than that, dating to classical times and attributable to others (such as John Hall and Marc Isambard Brunel, who deserve some of the credit for refining the idea in more modern times).

Eli Whitney had a lot of help–and still did not succeed at his stated goal

However, neither Whitney nor anyone else actually succeeded in making the idea of true "manufacturing" from standardized *interchangeable* parts practical until the 1850s. The long delay between the concept and its practical realization had several causes. Although Whitney et al. could design interchangeable parts, could make prototypes of those parts, and could show how useful that would be, what they could not do was reliably mass produce those parts or get anyone else to. The measurement standards of the time were not precise enough, nor was sufficient machining capability available, to make this possible.

In a nutshell, Whitney just didn't have the tools needed to make the tools needed to make the interchangeable parts. An entirely new industry–machine tools–had to be invented before Whitney's main idea of interchangeable parts could become a reality. But once those machine tools–and all of the standardized processes they required–became widely available every other form of manufacturing was soon revolutionized.

What emerged is now commonly called the "factory model." This factory model is not just about putting raw materials in at one end of a building and getting out finished product at the other end. After all, even the most hide-bound traditional craft-based "factory" could do that. No, it's about an entire science of breaking the products down into standardized parts, while breaking the production process down into standardized activities, all based on formal specifications. Moreover, this componentization of both parts and activities is applicable not just to assembly but to design, procurement, maintenance, and other areas.

And it's not just the end product that is ruthlessly componentized—it's the factory itself! Modern factories aren't just designed to produce one product, or even a predetermined set of products. Companies with those types of factories go out of business quickly, the first time the market for their particular product changes. Ergo, modern factories themselves must be able to change what they manufacture at will, albeit within certain boundaries. This means the factories themselves must be built from standardized parts, which can be changed or upgraded using standardized processes.

Current software development practices resemble those used by seventeenth-century craftsmen

So, what does all this have to do with today's notion of "software manufacturing"? Unfortunately, by any reasonable standard the typical IT shop is still stuck back in the craft-based world of manufacturing. That is, the specification, development, and deployment of each new solution is still a one-off project, whether we are starting from scratch or trying to integrate disparate systems. This is true even though we may use some fancy tools, sit in a modern office (the "factory"), and share some sophisticated technical infrastructure. From a modern "manufacturing" point of view, though, we still develop software not much differently than a group of craftsmen building custom firearms—one at a time—in a seventeenth-century munitions workshop.

How does this relate to MDA and the more modern vision of a "software factory"? In spite of the (at least) decade-old hype surrounding "reusable software components" and "assembling software," the truth is that nobody has yet been able to fully deliver on that vision. In practice, you either find vendor-proprietary sets of "components" or you don't get real components at all.

In any case, even the most advanced software developers today still spend an enormous amount of time and money patching together various tools, platforms, and existing applications to build the "components" they need and then to integrate them into a new solution. Most of them probably do not realize they are following in the footsteps of gunsmiths who wore out numerous files in making "standard" parts actually fit. The resulting modified "parts," of course, are even less "standard" than the originals.

Does that mean that the idea of a modern "software factory" can't be achieved? Not at all. It simply means is that the IT industry hasn't yet fully defined the notion of "machine tools" for software. Sure, we have some fancy development tools, but as yet they are not standardized to the point that they can be easily and reliably configured to produce "interchangeable parts" or "components" that can then reliably be combined into real solutions based on a set of formal specifications.

That's where MDA comes in. MDA is an approach that focuses on the standards and processes necessary to create true components and a reliable product life-cycle process for software through formal specifications. In terms of achieving industry-wide interoperability, MDA is still a work in progress. However, as these case studies amply illustrate MDA can already be used to figure out the best way for even a single company to architect a component-based strategy and to start transitioning toward a factory model for its entire software life cycle. Today, that MDA-based software factory might still have a few bottlenecks and shortcomings but at least we can identify and focus our efforts on removing them.

MDA focuses on the environment-the standards and processes-that enable the creation of software components

To extend the analogy a bit, we can loosely compare Whitney's achievements in the 1790s to the invention, some 200 years later, of interface definition languages (IDLs) in the software industry. That is, Whitney could show standard interfaces (interchangeable parts or components) and examples of those interfaces (prototypes). He could show how you could in theory make a system (a rifle) if you assembled those parts.

What he could not do with this equivalent of an IDL was reliably manufacture the components/parts that could support those interfaces. The inability to make those parts to the required tolerances in turn meant that there was no way to manage the "rifle life cycle" other than by taking a file to a lot of not-quite-interchangeable parts.

So, an IDL-style approach is necessary–but not sufficient–to support the factory model for software. The MDA standards, in contrast, provide a much more robust framework that will ultimately let us specify both the structure of a component and all of the associated semantics related to the way a component must function throughout its life cycle–a complete functional specification, if you will. The precise semantics of an MDA model correspond to the precise tolerances in a physical model because each determines whether the parts actually do what you want them to do–as opposed to simply appearing to fit together.

So, like the proprietary software vendors of today, Eli Whitney was able to show what could be done if you could make parts to certain specifications. He successfully demonstrated being able to shoot the gun assembled from (prototype) parts, replace a part, and then shoot again. At the time, it was an amazing feat, but there were too many missing standards and tooling technologies for the vision to be realized completely.

No matter how hard he tried, Whitney just could not build a factory–and he could not describe how anyone else could build a factory either. He could not describe a reliable process by which close-tolerance parts could be created, and he could not tell you how to build a machine that could reliably support the execution of such a process. More importantly, he did not yet even have a language with which to describe any of this.

New capabilities enable the creation of formerly unimaginable things, and we do not think that MDA is an exception to this rule

It took another 60 years to get to the point of a standardized manufacturing model, and then about another 70 years to perfect the end-to-end technology needed to support Whitney's big idea across a wide range of industries. By the 1920s, innovators such as Henry Ford had worked out enough of the technical and logistical kinks to support the production of automobiles–a far more complex process than anything Whitney was thinking about in 1790. But once that powerful blend of technology and logistics was generally understood, it ultimately enabled not only the mass production of rifles but of infinitely more complicated and sophisticated mechanisms. This is to be expected. New capabilities typically enable the creation of formerly unimaginable things.

We believe that MDA now provides the foundations for achieving all of these things in support of a true software factory. It has taken 15 years to get from IDL to MDA, so–even giving our industry credit for operating in "Internet time"–we are certainly still less than halfway to our ultimate goal of the universal software factory.

That is, we are still at an early stage in developing and applying MDA technology, and we should not be shocked that we don't yet have highly componentized interchangeable system modules available off the shelf for every kind of application. Fortunately, with the emergence of MDA we are finally at the point where we have a common language for defining true software components and for adequately describing the tools and processes necessary to create and assemble such components.

But look at what happened to the notion of the physical "factory" after it reached a similar point! Today there are many different types of factories: continuous process flow, factories that assemble parts from other factories, "lights-out" factories with little or no human presence, and so on. Visionaries are talking about factories that maintain themselves, and even factories that produce factories. With nano-manufacturing, the concept is being brought down to the molecular and even biological level. So, the general concept of the "factory" has grown along with our overall capabilities, and has been adapted to the specific needs of various industries.

MDA, although very general today, will branch into industry-specific specialties over time

It seems reasonable to expect the same sort of thing to happen to MDA technologies over time. As these case studies show, there are already many flavors of MDA in the real world today, including MDA for real-time systems, for embedded systems, for systems integration, and so on. We see no reason why this number shouldn't grow. Today, the general concept of MDA is still just being introduced to the software industry, along with some general MDA tools. But each industry always finds its own way of applying such things, just as industries applied the notion of a factory in different ways.

This "branching" of MDA was actually anticipated by the OMG, which assumed that many special interest groups (SIGs) and task forces (TFs) would emerge, each with its own flavor of MDA. As of this writing, there are already nine such MDA SIGs and TFs formally operating within the OMG: Business Enterprise Integration; Consultation, Command, Control, Communications, and Intelligence (C4I); Finance; Healthcare; Life Science Research; Manufacturing Technology and Industrial Systems (ManTIS); Software-based Communications; Space; and Transportation.

The case studies in this book are another type of real-life demonstration of this branching of MDA. They illustrate and inform us about all of the elements that go into using MDA to guide the building of business solutions in various environments. Because we are still in the relatively early stages of MDA's development, these case studies are perhaps the best way to present the emerging big picture, including which parts of that picture are not quite yet in focus.

When you read these case studies, you begin to see what people have to think about when they try to apply MDA to real-life problems. Someday, this will be second nature. Everyone will be attuned to modeling, to the process of modeling, and even to modeling the process of modeling, and so on. As the standards mature, more and more support will be built into the supporting "machine tools." Today, people still have to work their way through the overall approach and adapt it to their specific needs "by hand." But even so, these case studies show that they can still gain great advantages and benefits in the process of doing so.

Modeling will someday be second nature–to practitioners and tools

So this is where we are with respect to MDA today. The industry is still in the early introductory period of MDA adoption. We are at the point where, if you are willing to fill in some of the blanks yourself, there are some very interesting proto-tools available and great benefits to be gained by applying them correctly.

Eventually, the early adopters who take this approach will not only be continuously rewarded (that is already happening as we type) but will be moving faster than their competition in the global race toward a brave new model-driven world. They are already gaining hard-earned knowledge about what it takes to develop using an MDA-based approach. So, as the MDA tools and standards continue to improve these people will be in the best position to rapidly exploit those improvements as well.

These are exactly the types of things the people in our case studies have told us: "We realized the important things were people and process," and "We realized this would allow us to sell a whole different kind of product to our customers." More than anything else, these case studies are examples of organizations that in going through the process of adopting–and adapting–MDA are coming up with innovations that not only give them a competitive advantage but help drive the global MDA revolution.

Here's one final thought before you proceed to the case studies themselves. In this early phase of MDA's own development, its current rapid dissemination must be credited not only to the OMG, to the emerging class of MDA tool vendors, and of course to the brave end users but also to the many consultants who are now introducing their clients to the benefits of a model-driven approach. In each

Each case study showcases not only a satisfied end user but a dedicated consulting organization

of our case studies, there is not only a generally satisfied end user but also a dedicated professional services provider helping that end user learn the ropes and avoid the pitfalls that inevitably come with transitioning to a new approach.

At a higher level, these MDA consultants are playing a key role in making MDA work in the overall marketplace. Fortunately, very early in MDA's life cycle a group of such consultants took the step of banding together to create an OMG-sponsored program—MDA FastStart—specifically designed to help end users new to MDA begin their transition to a model-driven approach.

At this writing, the MDA FastStart program has grown to include more than 30 consulting organizations, each of whom the OMG recognizes as a Qualified Service Provider (QSP). Every one of the consultants involved in our case studies comes from this group of QSPs. As much as anyone else, their dedication to helping others learn about and correctly apply MDA is making a major contribution to the upcoming MDA revolution.

We want to personally thank those consultants, and their end users, for contributing their very valuable time and attention to this book. As you can imagine, none of these folks have a lot of free time to spare. Yet, for each case study they agreed to sit through several hours of interviews over a several-week period. In addition, each participant agreed to review the resulting transcripts and provide additional comments and clarifications. We hope you will agree with us that, judged by the results, it was time well spent.

2

CHAPTER TWO

COMPUWARE/STATE OF OHIO JOB AND FAMILY SERVICES

A state organization faces and overcomes some software development credibility issues, the system is delivered just as the requirements are officially signed off, and MDA adoption is done in "stealth mode."

BACKGROUND

Ohio's Job and Family Services organization had a federal mandate to implement a statewide Child Welfare Information system

The Job and Family Services (JFS) department of the Ohio State government has a sophisticated IT department with a budget of about $300 millon a year. Although they employ a large IT staff, they also look for ways to automate processes so that they can carry out the duties of government more efficiently. In 1993, the federal government mandated per-state software systems to support child welfare, and Ohio's Statewide Automated Child Welfare Information System (SACWIS) project was undertaken as a result of this mandate.

Dynamics Research Corporation (DRC) is a publicly held company, head-quartered in Andover, Massachusetts. DRC's primary mission is to deliver solutions and services to federal, state, and local government.

Compuware, founded in 1973, is a very large IT solutions company. Their OptimalJ product was introduced in 2001 as a J2EE developer productivity tool, and is now recognized as a leading implementation of MDA standards. Compuware is a long-time member of the OMG and an MDA Qualified Service Provider, and has contributed heavily to the creation of the OMG standards that form the foundation of MDA.

DRC was the prime contractor for the Ohio SACWIS project, with responsibility for overall project management and requirements. Compuware was responsible for the development of the system and conversion from the old system (unlike the federal government, the state of Ohio has no requirement that prevents a single vendor from undertaking any or all aspects of a single project).

WHY OHIO JFS CHOSE AN MDA APPROACH AND WHAT THEY HOPED TO ACHIEVE

For the State of Ohio JFS, adoption of an MDA approach did not spring primarily from a conscious decision to employ MDA. Their use of MDA was in part a side effect of the vendors they chose to help implement the SACWIS project.

JFS released a SACWIS request for information (RFI) in February of 2002. Several vendors responded, including six vendors who had experience in SACWIS implementations (in Wisconsin, West Virginia, Colorado, Maine, Indiana, and Montgomery County in Ohio).

JFS then released a request for proposal (RFP) to vendors in December of 2002. The major criteria for evaluating RFP responses were:

- *People:* SACWIS experience
- *Process:* How SACWIS will be developed
- *Product:* Proposed functional and technical solution

JFS chose DRC in part because DRC's people have been involved in SACWIS development/implementation since 1996, with both prime contractor and project-leading credentials. DRC's process is SEI/CMM Level 3 certified [DRC uses a customized version of the Rational Unified Process (RUP)]. In addition, DRC's "product" in this context includes their successful SACWIS implementations in other states. Angelo Serra, project manager for the JFS SACWIS project, described the path to an MDA-based project this way:

JFS chooses partners with impeccable credentials in software methodology and SACWIS implementation

> When we began the process, we realized that this would be a massive project and we knew that a number of other states had experienced difficulties in implementing similar projects. So, we knew that we would need something to jump-start our process. We had already begun researching MDA, and researching how some of the more agile software development processes could assist us in delivering what we had to deliver in a timely fashion.
>
> We had been given a deadline which, while not arbitrary, was certainly politically expedient. We had been given eighteen months by the director of the agency and we wanted to make sure that we had something that would allow us to deliver within that timeframe.
>
> As a result of the bidding process, the winning bidder–Dynamic Research Corporation–proposed an MDA model to guide the project. We had begun to move down this path in the first place, and the winning vendor arrived with a very polished way of proceeding down this path to implement it more effectively.

DRC in turn chose Compuware as their implementation partner, in part because Compuware had successfully implemented child welfare systems in Cuyahoga and Montgomery counties in Ohio. As it turned out, Compuware took the initiative of suggesting modifications to the RUP development methodology to include MDA, and this hybrid process was adopted after some refinement.

The SACWIS contract deliverables included the categories Project Management, Change Management, System Analysis and Design, Conversion, System Development, and System Testing. JFS realized that SACWIS was simultaneously a process initiative, a technology initiative, a people initiative, and an organizational initiative. More importantly, they realized that the most frequent reasons given for project failure have to do with people issues rather than technology issues.

Critical success factors: focus on business outcomes, broad executive involvement, change management, and a strong process

With DRC's help, they made explicit the factors they considered critical to success, which included focusing on business outcomes, broad executive involvement, careful attention to change management, strong process, and a strong team of decision makers. Their attention to change management was perhaps the most far-reaching part of their approach. JFS views change management as "promoting and fostering the awareness, acceptance, and implementation of SACWIS and the corresponding changes in business processes and workflows." This view was translated into a very strong and comprehensive program to keep stakeholders informed, to assess the organizational impediments to success, and to address those impediments in an open and forthright manner.

But what about MDA? On the one hand, the project documentation (see *http://jfs.ohio.gov/sacwis/*) clearly indicates that MDA is central to the development process, and Compuware's OptimalJ tool certainly has an MDA foundation.

On the other hand, the MDA-based technical and developmental aspects of the JFS SACWIS project, however important, are only one part of the efforts that made this project a success. Still, we were somewhat surprised by the answer Gary Dykstra, Global Client Advisory Board Manager at Compuware, gave when we asked what he thought about the client's opinion of MDA and the MDA experience, which follows.

MDA's presence in the process was not widely advertised at first...

You know, I spent all day with the customer yesterday, and we talked at length about the project, but the term *MDA* never came up. I think it is kind of transparent to the end user. They don't think along the lines of, "This is MDA and MDA is responsible for our success here." Certainly MDA was used here, and many of the benefits the customer might cite come from the MDA approach, but I don't know if there is a broad realization that MDA was at the heart of the success of the project.

I think that MDA is a paradigm shift and that its use will make all aspects of IT more successful. We have struggled with the notion of MDA from a marketing perspective from the very beginning. Do people like or not like MDA? Does mentioning MDA give us any leverage in the marketplace? Or do we just start making stuff that works and perhaps put in a footnote that says "MDA is what made this successful." Even in technology-driven organizations, they tend not to get down to the level of what's making it go.

There is food for thought here. Perhaps MDA will not be truly successful unless and until it is ubiquitous–and entirely "under the covers." Angelo Serra of JFS had a slightly different, though equally interesting, take on the matter. His comment was:

> One of the things I've learned from my experience in the government space is that if you come charging in and say something like "We are using the rational unified process" or "We are using MDA" or "We are using extreme programming" people will immediately run out and form an opinion about what that means. Good, bad, or indifferent, they will form an opinion and charge forward with it.
>
> And technical people, who tend to be very exacting and precise in order to deliver the products that they have to deliver, will try to do things precisely as specified in the approach or technology that's been announced. And if there is any departure from the canonical approach, as they understand it, they tend to throw a fit.
>
> So, you find yourself burning a lot of time convincing people that it doesn't necessarily have to be that way, and that these are guidelines rather than absolute rules. But these arguments are time consuming, and painful, and counterproductive.
>
> While there are a number of things we're doing that are very much MDA, we have not used that specific term in some cases. In fact, we have recently begun using the term *MDA* and telling people that they have been using it all along. They now realize that the modeling work done by various teams, in sequence but independently of each other (for example, PIM, then PSM), is all MDA.
>
> If we had started out by telling them we were doing MDA–they would have regarded it as yet another "flavor of the month" initiative from management. And they would have researched it to death and reached some perception of MDA overall. But they would not have understood all the individual pieces of the MDA process and how they fit together.
>
> But by having first worked through those individual pieces, they have now come to the realization that they are working with something bigger. Yes, it has the MDA name attached to it. And it is working! It is doing what it is supposed to do. And while it may not be "pure" MDA (if there is such a thing) it is certainly working for us.

...but MDA's benefits are now well understood

CHALLENGES

There are 88 counties in Ohio, each of which is responsible for the care of children. At the beginning of this statewide project, some of those counties had automated childcare support systems in place and some did not. The result was a patchwork environment of legacy procedures, proprietary per-county procedures, various paper-based systems, and legacy data in various forms–all of which had to be assimilated into the new SACWIS system.

Existing county systems had to be assimilated and federal-level technical and policy mandates had to be met—all on a very tight schedule

The State of Ohio approached the project by having a three-month rapid requirements definition phase, in which they considered the range of solutions/ systems that were in place, their various respective data models, an exhaustive list of use cases, and legacy systems whose functions had to be integrated or replaced. Of course, there were also federal requirements—in both the policy and the technical realm—that had to be met in order for the state to receive federal money.

One of the main motivations for adoption of an MDA approach was that when the Compuware team looked at the project proposal they realized it was very optimistic about what could be accomplished in the agreed-upon time frame—and the client had a firm fixed-price engagement in mind. Compuware argued that if the project was done using traditional development methods it was approximately 30% overcommitted before it even began. Thus, cutting development time was one of the main motivations for adopting MDA.

Change management and motivation of people are the keys

In addition, in the time since the 1993 federal government mandate for such statewide child welfare systems there had been numerous attempts by states to implement them. Some of these projects—notably in California, New York, and Florida—failed to meet their original schedules and budgets by large margins. The State of Ohio did not want an experience like that, and there was a great deal of pressure to get it right in light of these past failures. These issues were certainly going through the client's collective mind as they were figuring out how to get their SACWIS project done successfully.

Perhaps the most important challenge to be overcome by the JFS organization was dealing with change, including the technical changes required by the new web-based application style and the changes implied by working in tandem with vendor organizations to develop the code. Angelo Serra of JFS described how he prepared his group for these changes and motivated them to accept the challenges:

The perception of "state employees" was a potential issue

We had already begun preparing our group for a change. For example, we knew this was going to be a web-based system. We knew we would be using an updated version of the database on the back end. And we knew that we were not building a client server application. Instead, we were building a multi-tier application. So, we had already set up some of the basic training classes needed to cover these topics. For example, how web applications work, what is standard and what is not standard, as well as some basic coding and design principles for HTML and Java. We knew this sort of thing was coming at us because all the vendors who had given proposals up to that point had mentioned these things.

We then gathered up the IS staff, and had a very frank conversation with them. I said, "We have folks coming in from the private sector," and at that point there was the expected grumbling and groaning. I told them that they had a choice to make for today, as well as for the ensuing months of this project, because the people coming in from the outside may have a certain view of state workers. Often the perception of state workers is that of coffee-swilling, donut-munching, shovel-leaning group where you have five people watching and one person working.

I told them, "You will be a major part of our development team. And if you cannot show that you can add value to that team, to pull your own weight and add knowledge and skills to the effort of delivering SACWIS for the State of Ohio, you will be sidelined very quickly. Your choice today is to decide whether you have skills to bring forward to help make this happen, or not. And if you don't have those skills, the next question is whether you want to acquire those skills and bring them to the team to help make this work, or not."

I told them that if you don't want to do this, that's fine—I will help you move to a situation where you will be happy, and where you will have a career path, if you want to move on. But I said that I would rather not see anyone do that because I knew very well that everyone there on the IT side understands why we are here—we are here to help the kids in Ohio.

And the one great advantage that our group had, which may be somewhat uncommon in the government sector, is dedication to the mission. They're very committed to dealing with the issues of foster care, adoptive care, and child abuse/neglect issues. Everyone is. There are people within the group who are adoptive parents and foster care parents as well. Some have family members who are participating in this way and others were themselves in the system when they were younger. So they have a vested, personal interest in what is going on.

I then said, "You are going to make this decision. And if you decide to participate, I want to give you the tools that you need to become a productive member of the team." And every one of them opted in. They said they were in for a penny, in for a pound, and ready to go.

The JFS IT staff accepts the challenge

EXPANDING GOALS (OR LACK THEREOF)

It is fairly common for goals (project goals, organizational goals, enterprise goals) to expand as users become more familiar with MDA and what it can achieve. However, after seeing the extensive up-front work JFS undertook—both in requirements gathering and project scoping—we suggested to Angelo Serra that the SACWIS project was already so big and risky that there really wasn't much room for expanding goals. His reply follows.

No, there wasn't. The federal people paid us a big compliment, though I found it kind of frightening. They had to approve our RFP before we published it, and they said that we had done an awesome job of putting together our requirements ahead of time. And being the skeptical people we are, we couldn't help but ask, "What did everyone else do?" Because we knew very well that we still had a lot more to do. There is always some ambiguity in requirements. You never have time to nail down the requirements as well as you would like, and we felt some trepidation about ours.

We had a couple of curveballs thrown at us in the project, but for the most part we were prepared for almost everything that occurred because we had spent so much time, not only in talking with the policy people at the state level but also in

A compliment from the federal people

discussions with various other teams to understand the various needs of the county and how they relate to the needs of the entire state.

We took their input on these requirements and even took the extra step of distributing the requirements document back to them and asking them whether we had gotten it right. The requirements that went into the RFP were based on the seventh or eighth revision of that document.

But even then, the machinery of the state does not sit still. We significantly changed our risk and safety assessment model–how we look at families and children at risk in the state, and their level of safety. There are two distinct models: actuarial and clinical. The actuarial model is very simplistic, with a laundry list of questions whose answers are numerically weighted. You answer the questions and calculate the total, and if you are over a certain number then there is a risk, and if you are under there is no risk.

That works well in large counties with a high turnover of caseworkers who don't have the clinical background needed to make judgments. The clinical model requires descriptions of the home condition, of the interrelationships between the adults and children in the family, of the school situation, and so on. These are broad and soft questions that, unless the caseworker has a lot of experience, will be difficult to answer. There are many people who believe in this clinical model–that you have to spend time with a family in order to understand the dynamics.

The SACWIS project provides the opportunity to debate an actuarial versus clinical approach

And for years we had put off the debate over which model is best for the State of Ohio. When SACWIS came along, we decided it was time to address this model question. We came up with a hybrid model, put together here in Ohio, which is unique to the 50 states. We are being watched by a number of other states, and are starting to pilot this model outside of the SACWIS application and model. There is another team within the policy office that is running this project. But, we had to put in a change order to get this hybrid model into the first version of our SACWIS project, and that was very painful–perhaps the single biggest modification we had to deal with–and this reflects how well the requirements team did their jobs.

HOW MDA WAS USED

MDA and agile software development are complementary ideas

One of the interesting aspects of this case study was its combining of a rigorous MDA-based process and agile development. Many projects experience some level of tension between those who believe in the importance of process rigor in determining schedule tracking, productivity metrics and so on, versus those who see process as an impediment to getting things built. Some in the IT industry have even argued that these two things are mutually exclusive.

The results of this case study rebut this argument. They support the notion that agile development and MDA are complementary, and even have a synergistic effect when used together. The idea that MDA and agile development are complementary boils down to this: A major tenet of agile programming is the importance of creating working software as soon as possible.

This is achieved by short development iterations, each followed by a check with the business community to determine the correctness/validity of the iteration's output. The advantage of using an MDA-compliant tool for code generation is that you can achieve short development/implementation iterations more easily with MDA. And these iterations have much more business logic content because so much of the low-level code is automatically generated, allowing the development team to focus on providing application functionality.

We asked Vasil Hlinka, Compuware Project Manager for the SACWIS project, about this particular point because other case study participants had told us that in a typical large project only 15% of coding tasks are really of interest to programmers (the rest being low-level drudgery). Thus, one of the real advantages of MDA and associated code generation is that developers can concentrate on the 15% of project code that implements interesting things such as business logic and algorithms. Vasil agreed with the thrust of this statement, although he said that he thought the proportion of interesting code was more like 40% on this project.

MDA is an enabler for the use of agile software development techniques on large projects

> In a sense, this 60/40 split is what actually allows agile programming to be used for large projects—but where it is appropriate rather than everywhere. I think the agile methodologies are very good for small teams and small projects (five to eight people).
>
> In that situation, you might not need the rigor that MDA brings. But if you want to build an enterprise system that involves the interrelations and complexities of a statewide child welfare system, this is the way to enable agile methods to work on a large project.
>
> I would add that I think that MDA, and in particular the OptimalJ tool, were key enablers for the use of agile development techniques on this project. OptimalJ provided the necessary structure and cohesion down to the code level, which proved invaluable to our effort, especially during the late phases of the project.

In this project, requirements definition/refinement, system design, and the development iterations themselves were driven by rapid requirements definition (RRD) sessions and joint application design (JAD) sessions. The following descriptions of these processes were taken from the SACWIS page on the State of Ohio's web site (*http://jfs.ohio.gov/sacwis/*).

> Rapid Requirements Definition: The purpose of the RRD Sessions is to establish the baseline requirements for SACWIS by clarifying and verifying the Systems Requirements Document (SRD) that was developed by the Business Partners Group (county and state staff) and the SACWIS Assessment Review Guide (SARGe) that was developed by the Administration for Children and Families.
>
> Joint Application Design & Development: The design and development of Ohio SACWIS uses an "iterative" approach. The large business processes are divided into smaller, logical pieces. Each piece comes to life through the Joint Application Design and Development (JAD) process. The JAD Sessions elaborate each use

Rapid requirements definition and joint application design and development processes were central to the success of the project

case (e.g., Worker Creates Intake Referral) developed in the Rapid Requirements Definition (RRD) Session to create the details necessary to develop the software components (i.e., Inputs, Outputs, Detailed Business Rules).

The workings of the RRD and JAD processes, described in more detail in the material following, were central to the success of the project. As Gary Dykstra of Compuware put it:

> What we were able to employ on this project, and facilitated by use of the tool in automating code generation, was that they were able to have a working build every two weeks. At the end of each two-week iteration they could check in with the business and ask them if it was what they wanted, whether the use cases were implemented correctly, etc.
>
> So, there was a constant, and short, feedback loop between the developers and the business stakeholders. It was not at all like the old approach where you develop for eighteen months behind closed doors and roll out the result only then for user approval. There was constant checking with the business.
>
> In the event, the rigor was at the architectural level. The MDA approach and the tooling facilitated that, in the sense that the architecture is codified in the tool, and in the transformation patterns that transform a PIM to a PSM, and a PSM to generated code.
>
> But note that the agile development took place in the business logic implemented by individual developers. As you build out the business logic, and do the development work that cannot be automated, that is where you employ agile process at the development level. But at the architectural level you have the rigor and control, as well as the metrics needed by management.
>
> This project almost looks like the old waterfall methodology, but when you get down to the implementation of a business use case by a programmer you see the agile development processes: working in small teams, paired programming, collaboration, quick iterations, face-to-face meetings, and all the tenets of agile programming. But this is part of the larger framework that offers management what they need as well.

The project did not create a formal CIM, although the output of the RRD sessions can be characterized as baseline business models. During the requirements capture phase, a modeling specialist from Compuware was involved, which resulted in high-level business models and refinement of these models in subsequent RRD iterations.

The RRD process defines project scope, while the JAD process fleshes out the details

The purpose of the RRD sessions was to "scope out the project" by determining the number of use cases to be implemented, and then to create preliminary/rough descriptions of these use cases. After that was done, the JAD iterations began, each of which was on a strict 10-day schedule. Each JAD iteration took the rough use cases created during RRD and fleshed out the details.

The tight schedule demanded an organization in which five teams worked concurrently and independently on different functional aspects of the application.

Each of the five teams spent a 10-day JAD iteration on a set of use cases, with the intent of completing the use cases and their high-level designs and then getting the stakeholders to sign off that the use cases were complete and the design met the requirements.

Upon completion of the JAD iteration, the work specified was put on the construction queue. The construction team, which was also working on 10-day iterations (offset by one, of course) took finished designs and use cases from the queue and begin building them, again in an iterative fashion, and these implementation iterations included the creation of PIM and PSM and the generation of code. The relationship of the JAD and implementation iterations (as well as the associated quality control and management functions) is shown in Figure 2.1.

10-day iterations of RRD, JAD, and construction phases

Although the iterative requirements/design/development processes described previously seem straightforward, there was one very unusual aspect of this in the SACWIS project. The requirements that drove the design and implementation were not officially signed off by the client until the first quarter of 2006–more than 18 months after the project began, when the system was about to start the User Acceptance Testing phase! We discovered this fact while we were interviewing Vasil Hlinka of Compuware in early December of 2005. We asked him about the MDA-related factors that allowed the team to succeed with a schedule that was clearly too optimistic for traditional development approaches. His answer:

Requirements are formally signed off–at about the same time coding is completed

> MDA, coupled with the iterative development approach that we put together, have been a key component to our success. We are currently in the sixth week of system test, and roughly the eighteenth month of the project. The functional spec, which represents requirements, was submitted to the client a few weeks back. It represents the sum total of use cases, requirements, report specs, and screen specs that have been developed during the JAD sessions. This was formally put before the client only a few weeks ago.
>
> Because we have been working with the State, with its many constituents, getting consensus on requirements is very, very difficult. So, only now have we been able to submit the requirements for formal sign-off. Technically, at this point we should be sitting around a table and discussing whether we should start coding in January, now that we've finally got final requirements in place.
>
> Rather than doing that, we are seriously considering giving the client a finished product for formal user acceptance in January! That's a huge contrast. But with MDA and incremental development we have been able to simultaneously build consensus on the requirements, and build the application, in an iterative fashion. So, many of the benefits that you read about with MDA have come to fruition here, especially the ability to nail down requirements in a very difficult environment. I can't say enough about the benefits of MDA, not only for us but for the client as well.

Nailing down requirements in a very difficult environment

When we interviewed Angelo Serra in January of 2006, we asked whether the requirements had yet been officially signed off. His response was as follows.

Project Approach - Iteration Approach

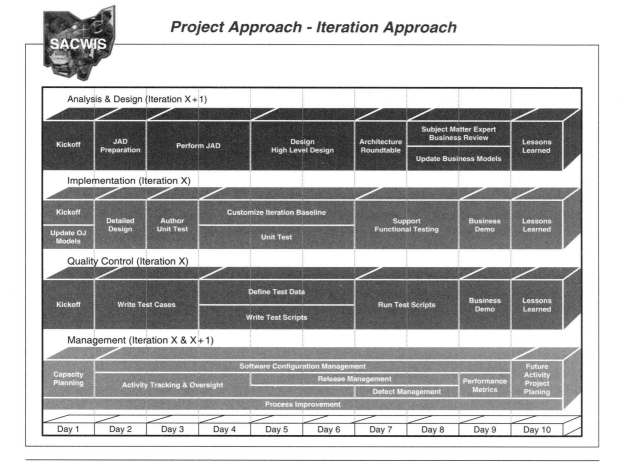

FIGURE 2.1 Iterative development process.

The requirements feedback process is expanded and reapplied to system testing

We have signed off on those requirements. As is the case in any large project, especially in the user acceptance phase, we are finding things to tweak. We're finding that some of the things created in JAD sessions, and which were thought to be captured in the requirements, in fact were not captured and did not make it into the application.

There are perhaps seven or eight of these things and we are now going back to update the document, bring them forward in use cases, and give them to development. So, the same feedback processes used in the JAD and RRD sessions are being expanded and reapplied to system test.

We are not deviating from the previous process, which is now very comfortable to people. Our requirements feedback process is like a security blanket. By reusing these processes, people have a basis to work from, and the comfort that it has worked in the past.

We then asked for an example of something that had to be tweaked, and how that was handled. Angelo replied as follows.

One was the address function. We have a complex process to get an address into the system, checking that it is correct for the postal service, et cetera. What we initially modeled was at too high a level, and after starting user acceptance testing we found situations that had not been foreseen. There were two loops where testers found themselves reentering addresses over and over, to no effect.

We reopened that model, retraced the address-capture steps based on the user feedback, to see what was going wrong. Right now, we have one vendor developer and one of my guys working on the problem and how to streamline the process. They are scheduled to generate code tomorrow, and we should see the results in a build next week.

This kind of thing would have taken 14 to 21 days before MDA, instead of the seven or so days it takes now. In the old days we would have first walked through the code, created a model from it (for example, on a whiteboard), and had people weigh in on the technical aspects. We would then invite the business people, bring them up to speed on what was happening, and then together decide what to do.

In this case, we already had a model with a direct connection down to the code, so we did not have to worry about back-and-forth reconciliation between model and code to ensure that the model was correct. We could look at the model, make our decisions from it, and then have people look at the implementation for validation that the requirements had been met successfully, or to produce an updated plan for necessary modifications. The model would then be modified, code generated, and out pops the new version.

Tweaking a function–yesterday versus today

We ventured that this back-to-front approach to requirements was somewhat risky for both the consulting companies and the client organization. Back in the old days, you had to have the requirements nailed down and signed off so that everyone was "covered," so to speak. We asked Angelo Serra about this risk. He commented as follows.

Yes, we all took some level of risk in this. We did make sure that we had check points along the way where we could measure progress, and we encouraged people very strongly to think hard about things up front, and discouraged people from changing their minds about requirements without very good reason.

But we did all take a risk by doing it this way. Was it a huge risk? I don't think so. Had other groups done this before? Probably not, at least not within this state. Our group does tend to take some risks because otherwise we wouldn't get anything done. But it is possible that some people would look at what we've done and call it crazy, and say that there was no way it could succeed.

Justifying the risk of simultaneously defining requirements and implementing the system

We then asked Angelo whether he had ever found himself in front of a more senior manager, answering the question, "How can you possibly go ahead with this project when the requirements aren't even settled?" He laughed and said:

> Yes we did. And this is perhaps another advantage of using MDA. By the time you are able to publish the higher-level models you can also describe how you will go about implementing them. You can demonstrate that you are not simply shooting from the hip, and that you are following a process that you have every reason to believe will work.
>
> You can show someone the necessary feedback loops, the checkpoints, activities, et cetera. And once people saw that we had taken the time to plan this carefully, once they saw the plan, they had some level of assurance that we knew what we were doing and would succeed. In other words, it was not a case of us saying, "Just trust us, this will work."

PROCESS AND TOOLS

Although the State of Ohio SACWIS project did not begin with a proof-of-concept or pilot, Compuware had previously participated in another project for the JFS organization, and that project used Compuware's OptimalJ tool. However, at that time OptimalJ was less mature than it is today. Although the client was pleased with the delivered application, the problems encountered in the course of that project drove a lot of discussion about whether OptimalJ was appropriate to use for in the SACWIS project.

JFS, DRC, and Compuware jointly create a modified software development process

For prime contractor DRC, and for JFS, the methodology of choice was the Rational Unified Process (RUP). JFS was a bit nervous about the newness of MDA itself and about the new version of the OptimalJ tool. They wanted to mitigate their risks, and one of their mitigation strategies was to require that their high-level business models be done in Rose. Another requirement was that JBuilder should be used in addition to OptimalJ. Here again they were just covering all the bases.

However, Compuware representatives suggested some modifications to the RUP process, and refined that process further in discussions with both JFS and DRC. In the end, the project adopted this modified process. In an arrangement similar to that of the JAD teams, there were five development teams, one for each functional area.

- *Team* 1: Intake and Investigation, Person Management, Central Registry
- *Team* 2: Case Management, Court, and Adoption
- *Team* 3: Resource Management

- *Team 4*: Administration (Staff Management, Alerts and Ticklers, Security, Case Assignment and Transfer, Reports Framework)
- *Team 5*: Financial Management, Eligibility, and Interfaces

In addition, a sixth team was organized after a few iterations had been completed. The sixth team worked on technical use cases–infrastructure pieces that did not map to any particular functional requirement for the application.

The six development teams were on a strict 10-day implementation iteration schedule. Day 1 of a development iteration always started with a review of the iteration plan. Days 2 and 3 were devoted to mapping the high-level design produced by the JAD session–in the form of Rose models, VOPCs ("view of participating class" diagrams), data dictionaries, and some flow diagrams–into OptimalJ.

OptimalJ provides two kinds of models. One is the business-centric Domain Model, which is free of technology details and equivalent to an MDA PIM (Platform-Independent Model). Once the Domain Model is complete, OptimalJ automatically transforms it to an Application Model, which is equivalent to an MDA PSM (Platform-Specific Model), and it is targeted to the J2EE platform. The transformation from Domain Model to Application Model is mediated by OptimalJ's Technology Patterns.

Modeling with Compuware's OptimalJ tool

When developing or enhancing an OptimalJ Domain Model, designers can define business rules in a declarative way. All Domain Model definitions are reused and inherited by the lower-level Application Models and the actual code. Thus, the more that is defined in the Domain Model, the more detail in the Application Model and the more code generated automatically.

Therefore, implementation teams would create a detailed design from JAD artifacts, using the OptimalJ tool to build a PIM that implemented the logical design as specified in the Rose model created by the JAD team. Each development team had a modeler (they were called Enterprise Java Beans (EJB) developers), who was the senior developer responsible for modeling and for use of the OptimalJ tool and code generation. The evolution of these models is shown in Figure 2.2.

When the detailed design was complete, some additional coding was done in the business tier and other tiers. Each team also had one or two Java/JSP developers who were primarily responsible for web tier coding and the Java action classes and JSPs used in the Struts environment–essentially, all of the presentation-tier work that supported the OptimalJ-generated code. The senior developer would then generate code, and that code would be released to the rest of the development team for further work.

On day 9 or thereabout, the developers would finish up and tag their work in preparation for the build/deploy step on day 10. On day 10, they performed a build and deployed the result. In the early iterations, some deployment issues needed to be addressed at that point, but the teams were usually able to avoid this in later iterations. The last step of the 10-day schedule was a "lessons learned" session, followed by preparation for the next iteration.

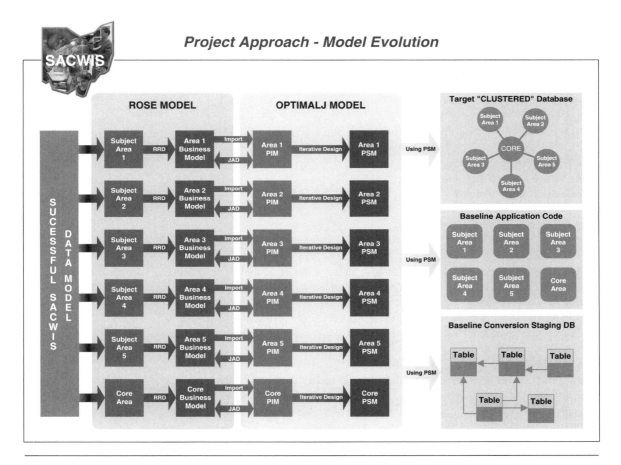

FIGURE 2.2   Model evolution.

DIVISION OF LABOR

The State of Ohio's SACWIS Integrated Project Team consisted of the following.

- State Management Information Systems and Business Project staff
- The DRC/Compuware team
- County IT and subject matter experts
- State subject matter experts
- More than 100 state IT staff

The RRD teams consisted of the following.

- County subject matter experts
- State subject matter experts
- Project business analysts
- Contractor business analyst

The JAD team included the RRD participants and added the following.

- Project programmer/analyst
- Contractor J2EE architecture lead
- Project testing specialist
- Contractor testing specialist
- Automated systems trainer
- Contractor training specialist

The development teams varied in size from five to eight developers (most teams had five members, and on these teams there were typically two JFS employees). Again, each development team had a modeling expert–a senior developer who was also responsible for use of the OptimalJ tool and code generation. Each team also had one or two Java/JSP developers who were primarily responsible for web tier and Struts coding.

Composition of development teams

The SACWIS project team created the marvelous pictures shown in Figures 2.3 and 2.4, which respectively capture the division of labor over the entire project schedule and the various development techniques used along the way.

Angelo Serra estimated that the core JFS team consisted of 13 developers and three managers on the technical side, and 18 analysts on the business side, but this does not include all of the SMEs (subject matter experts) who were brought in to help at various times. At its peak, the JFS headcount for the entire project was 136, while at its lowest point it was perhaps 40 (which is also the planned staffing level for post-implementation support).

PROJECT EXPERIENCE

In addition to the challenges that were obvious at the outset of the project, other challenges were encountered along the way. That is no surprise in a project this large, but what is surprising is the fact that they weathered these problems–such as major functionality changes, significant staff turnover, and the generally chaotic process of introducing a new methodology in a large project whose development staff was unfamiliar with MDA–with very little impact to the schedule or the functionality delivered.

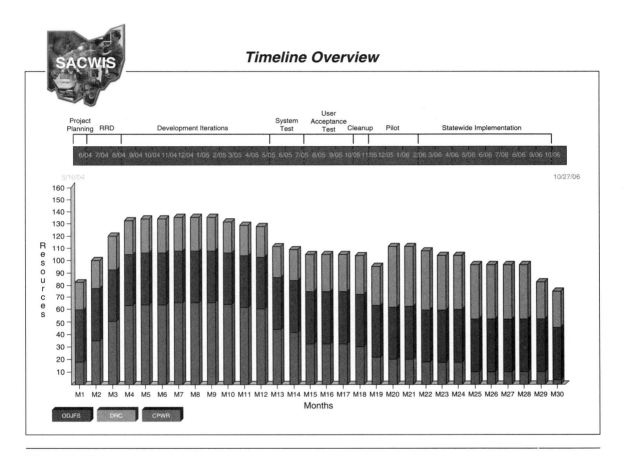

FIGURE 2.3 Timeline and division of labor.

We asked Vasil Hlinka, Compuware Project Manager for the SACWIS Project, why these change requests occurred and how the team handle them. His response follows.

Mid-project changes, small and large

There were a great many small change requests that did not register as "official" change requests but were still accommodated. As for the major ones, they had to do with what are called "architectural use cases." We tried to convince our partner and the client that such use cases have to be assigned a priority based on a technical as well as a business perspective.

Security was something we wanted to tackle very early on. And there were some key business use cases that were core to the application, which we said needed to be done early in the project. Unfortunately, for a number of reasons security was

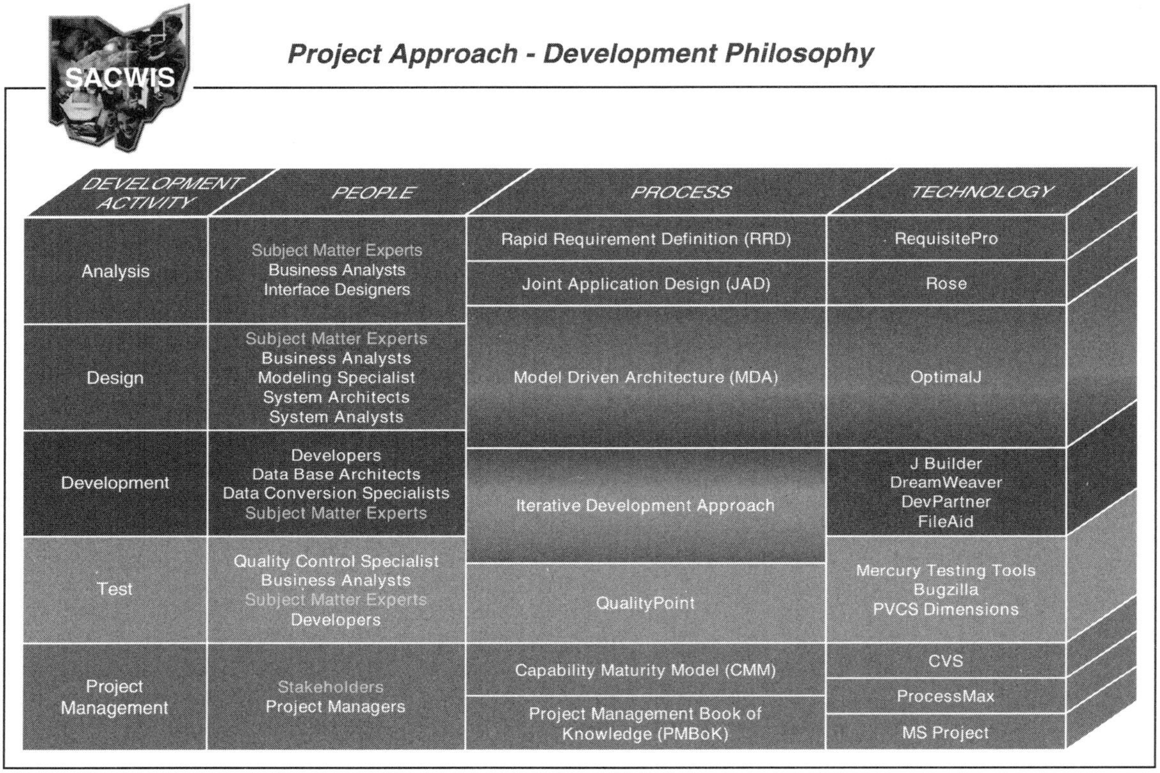

SACWIS

Project Approach - Development Philosophy

DEVELOPMENT ACTIVITY	PEOPLE	PROCESS	TECHNOLOGY
Analysis	Subject Matter Experts Business Analysts Interface Designers	Rapid Requirement Definition (RRD)	RequisitePro
		Joint Application Design (JAD)	Rose
Design	Subject Matter Experts Business Analysts Modeling Specialist System Architects System Analysts	Model Driven Architecture (MDA)	OptimalJ
Development	Developers Data Base Architects Data Conversion Specialists Subject Matter Experts	Iterative Development Approach	J Builder DreamWeaver DevPartner FileAid
Test	Quality Control Specialist Business Analysts Subject Matter Experts Developers	QualityPoint	Mercury Testing Tools Bugzilla PVCS Dimensions
Project Management	Stakeholders Project Managers	Capability Maturity Model (CMM)	CVS
			ProcessMax
		Project Management Book of Knowledge (PMBoK)	MS Project

FIGURE 2.4   Project approach and development philosophy.

left to the very end. The very core of the business behavior of the application was also left to the very last use cases developed. And finally, because of scheduling issues the reports specification was late. We argued that the report specs had to be done concurrently with the use cases, because you can't verify your inputs without checking the report output.

But all of these challenges were imposed on the project. You can imagine the difficulties of waiting until the end of the project to do security. And it was not a simple security scheme. It was role-based security with a great deal of flexibility in the final design. In addition, the specific business task the user was undertaking affected his security credentials. All this happened very late in the project, but we were able to accommodate and absorb these changes without significantly affecting the schedule.

There were a few changes requested by the client that resulted in scope changes. For those we put in official change orders, and got additional resources and monies for them. By the time the security design was nailed down, we had already built approximately 40% of the screens. So, there were two additional iterations paid for by the customer to accomplish that retrofit.

We then asked what it was about the process that allowed the team to solve these problems. Was it the agile aspect? Was there some MDA-related characteristic that allowed the team to overcome these difficulties? Vasil responded as follows.

The consistency and efficiency of MDA-based tooling increases project throughput

It was actually a combination of those two. For the majority of use cases, once the development team received them for a given iteration there were inevitably follow-up questions, changes, and clarifications. These were indeed accommodated by the agility of the process itself.

But in addition to that, having an MDA-based tool gave us additional consistency and efficiency, and that certainly helped us absorb these changes with minimal schedule impact. In the last iteration, we were pumping out a very large number of very difficult use cases.

I'm convinced that we could never have sustained that throughput without having a mechanism that let us generate the CRUD code—pretty much worry-free because of the OptimalJ tool—so that we could focus on the screens, the business rules, and so forth.

There were also mid-course corrections that had to be applied to the JAD process. The first few JAD iterations were described as "fairly chaotic" because JAD training had to accommodate new participants and stakeholders, and in some cases they did not really understand the notion of iterations or what the JAD process itself was all about.

Shakedown results in adjustments to the process

In the early iterations, many aspects of the design were of course subject to change. A side effect of accommodating these changes was that some process problems were identified and the team made a number of adjustments in response. For example, the initial development/construction process very optimistically assumed that testing would be done "just in time." That is, the first few days of modeling were to be followed by some coding, and the last few days of the iteration were to be allocated to having the QA (quality assurance) team test the code destined for the build of that iteration.

The team quickly found out that there was too much overhead in the testing process to achieve this goal. They adjusted the process so that the testing team worked on the previous iteration, rather than on the one undergoing construction by the development team.

Adjustments were made in the process of inter-team coordination as well. At first, the team employed an architecture "round table" meeting to review the high-level design created by the JAD sessions. However, they found that they had to set up an additional round table meeting to allow the modelers to address inconsistencies in the way various PIMs were created, and to coordinate the creation of services shared among multiple models. These coordination processes were put in place for the fourth and subsequent iterations.

Although the overall development process worked very well, other mid-course corrections were made. For example, each development team was seated together in the same area. Business analysts worked in same facility, and were "within shouting distance" of the developers–and by all accounts, development teams viewed that as a good thing.

Another very positive aspect of the development process was that the client developers were fully integrated within the development teams. A common problem in projects like this is that once the application is built the client may have difficulty taking it over for maintenance. But in this case, client developers were first-class citizens in the development team from the very beginning. They are now fully productive and capable of accepting the handoff from Compuware. Vasil Hlinka said:

Development teams composed of JFS and vendor personnel were completely integrated

> The majority of them were not even really Java developers when we started. J2EE is complex enough, and this is a very complex J2EE application. So, they were on a steep learning curve throughout, and this is another example of the benefits of this methodology.
>
> They were brought up to speed with no measurable impact on the overall productivity of the teams. Part of that was because we applied some of the notions of pair programming and some aspects of XP [eXtreme Programming] as well.
>
> Pair programming has different connotations–this was certainly not the variety where you have two coders who share a workstation and trade off the "driving." But there are some very positive aspects of pair programming which we did apply.

Angelo Serra of JFS told an amusing story (after ensuring that no names would be used) that illustrates the interchangeability of technical contributors from JFS and the vendors.

> The telling point for me came after one of the change orders. A vendor representative told me this story, in order to make sure I heard it from him and would not be upset. He said, "We need a couple of extra days to put together the Statement of Work for this change order," and I responded that this would not be a problem.
>
> He then said, "Well, I have a problem. I have this draft Statement of Work and I realized that some of the people on it are State of Ohio employees. I really don't think that you would go along with me billing you for the use of your own people!
>
> But this conversation alone tells you that all of our developers stepped up. They stood behind the answer to that question we asked them almost two years ago today. Essentially, while we weren't looking our guys became interchangeable with the vendor developers. And they now have the confidence necessary to really move things forward.

Although there were instances where people on a development team were not getting along and had to be shifted around, team membership in general remained constant and the teams worked well together. There was one major shift during the very last iterations, when some negative dynamics were noticed and addressed. An example of this would be an attitude of "We're doing our piece correctly, and while we notice some issues with code from other teams we're not going to spend any time in highlighting the issue or in helping fix their problems because we're just worried about our piece."

In another case, one of the teams (in a very critical area) was struggling and in general making things more difficult for themselves. This was noticed because of the large proportion of custom code created by that group. Project management addressed this issue by swapping team leads and members, thus changing the makeup of the problem team. This helped with the transfer of knowledge throughout the staff, and provided a better balance of technical aptitudes across the application teams.

Staff turnover is a problem to overcome

The problem of staff turnover was caused mainly by external events outside the control of the project team. Because so much training would be required, the project was staffed rapidly. But much to their chagrin, project management found that by the start of the first iteration they had already experienced about a 15% turnover. And at the time of this writing, staff turnover was 56%!

We asked Vasil Hlinka of Compuware about the cause of this undeniably high rate of turnover. He said:

> We had a bit of bad luck on this project, in part because the job market in the region got very hot. We had lined up some of the most talented Java people in the area for this project, and the attrition affected some of our best staff. In fact, some of the people in whom we invested the most time and training, and on whom we planned to rely, ended up leaving before we started the iterations.
>
> By any measure, we have run into more than our share of potholes on this road. But this is another reason for us to be very happy with the MDA process and the results we've achieved.

ORGANIZATIONAL DEVELOPMENT

We always ask case study participants about the effect of MDA adoption on the client's organization. The answer we got in this case is a bit unusual. In essence, a new organizational arrangement was consciously crafted as part of the delivery of this project. In other words, they did not try to fit the tooling and MDA into an organizational structure. Instead, they built the team to suit the project.

Organizational structure is driven by project needs

In this case the client divided the application into five functional areas so that they could divide 40 developers into teams of five to eight for each area, a tenet of agile development. The theory is that communication breaks down if you have more than that number of people working on one thing.

But those five functional areas had to work together to deliver an application, so there had to be some common oversight as well. Thus, a joint application development team was added, with separate responsibilities over the course of the two-week iterations. Their job was to oversee the application as a whole and to work on infrastructure pieces that spanned multiple functional areas, in order to support interdependencies among those areas.

Compuware's experienced project leaders and development leaders tried to accommodate the client's wishes with respect to tooling and process. And their experience was helpful in the creation of the successful organizational structure.

But some tweaks were tried along the way. For example, at first they co-located business analysts with the development teams, but that didn't "flow well" and the two groups were separated (but remained physically close enough for continuous communication). They also swapped people in and out of teams because of various personality issues. But the fact that the organization had enough built-in flexibility to make such changes dynamically was very important.

At the end of every two-week iteration, each of the six development teams spent a day examining "lessons learned" during that iteration. They discussed the problems they encountered, how things were working in general, and what could be done better. So, this wasn't a case of figuring out improvements in spare moments but was part of the process.

Examination of "lessons learned" is part of the process

"Organizational development" refers to the people in an organization as well as organization itself. Angelo Serra of JFS described some of the approaches JFS used to further the development of individual JFS contributors after the project was started.

In the context of the way the state does things, you get to a point where you know the issuing of a contract is imminent. At that point you can begin to figure out when various things will occur. From that point, as we got more information about what approaches and tools and versions would be used in the project we set about not only procuring necessary training for everyone but also setting up study groups for people within the project.

For example, we got copies of the "Gang of Four" patterns book[1] for everyone on the project, and one of the study groups was dedicated to a discussion of this. Once a week we would get together to dig through the patterns to gain a better understanding of them, and figure out how they might be used in the course of the project, as well as whether and how we might have used these patterns already in the past. Other study groups included one to understand the Java language, which

---

1   Erich Gamma, Richard Helm, Ralph Johnson, and John Vlissides. *Design Patterns: Elements of Reusable Object-oriented Software.* New York: Addison-Wesley Professional, 1995, ISBN: 0201633612.

we knew we would need, as well as Java server pages which deliver HTML on the back end.

I myself took on the design patterns study group, though I probably had no business doing so. But I did the same reading everyone else did, and brought my questions to the group along with theirs, and we spent an hour and a half each week working through them to reach a better understanding.

For the developers—and we have some very resourceful people—we found four fairly beefy desktop machines that were allocated to the group, and which we set up as a "sandbox" so that people could start programming in Java, doing JSP work, setting up the database, application server, and web server, and running the architecture in a limited fashion. Two people went out and got their Java programming certification from Sun. And this was all before the official start of the project.

So, I think we are doing pretty well. We have our faults and foibles, but our success speaks to the dedication and focus of the team we have. And their dedication is not to whiz-bang technical features but rather to the delivery of a useful case worker system to the State of Ohio, and they all understand that.

ONGOING AND PLANNED USE OF MDA

We asked Angelo Serra of JFS about any plans for using MDA for other projects within JFS. His response was that he expects that MDA will be used in an upcoming Medicaid application.

We have been talking with other groups within JFS. There have already been other efforts, much like ours, in other small pockets. One of the larger efforts that may benefit is that of a new Medicaid application. We are in the process of seeking bids on this, and have already put out an RFP from various vendors, but I think MDA will figure prominently in that.

This will definitely be an important proof point, because this Medicaid application will be an order of magnitude larger than the SACWIS project we are doing. So, it will be even more important for the Medicaid project to be up to speed and know what is going on in this process.

They will be using MDA because of the various technologies that must be brought to bear and integrated for this Medicaid system. Obviously, there will be heavy mainframe-based transaction processing on the back end, but they will also want to take advantage of a web front end, either via Java or .NET, to get information to various classes of users, either internally to state employees or externally to citizens of the State of Ohio.

And they will also want to build XML interfaces for interaction with various other systems. So this will really be a massive effort, and if I were a betting man I'd bet that this is where MDA will pop up next for us.

We then asked how the MDA message was being received elsewhere within the State of Ohio. Angelo said:

> I'm not sure I can speak to that, because a lot of those changes happen outside of my purview. I do think that one organizational dynamic that we will see more of is trying to educate teams ahead of time instead of as they go along, and not just on the technical side but also on the policy side.
>
> Our policy and business partners are working hand in hand with us to develop the SACWIS application, and they have gone through a significant amount of work to prepare their people; for example, to understand what it is like to work with a contractor and to understand some of the technical wrinkles we are dealing with.
>
> I think we will see this more and more, not only in the Medicaid application but also in a child care application that will soon be rewritten. We are already starting down that path on both the business and technical sides, making sure they understand how they need to capture and then flesh out their requirements.
>
> So, we are starting to see a movement, almost a grassroots movement on a project-by-project basis, that MDA looks like a good thing to do, so let's make sure our people are as prepared as we can make them.
>
> In the past, it was more of an "on-the-job training" approach, and the reason for this is that we don't have a huge training budget, and we've been careful not to burn it up unless we can see a direct benefit. But the SACWIS project has indeed shown a direct relationship and a benefit between the training we got and what we were able to produce.

TABLE 2.1　Project Profile: Statewide Automated Child Welfare Information System

Company/Organization	*Name:* State of Ohio Job and Family Services (JFS).
	Industry/Function: Support for all of Ohio's state and local child welfare agencies, covering a population of more than 11.5 million people across 88 counties.
	Project Size and Duration: 80 to 130 participants; 18 months.
	Geographical Extent: State of Ohio, USA.
	URL: http://jfs.ohio.gov/sacwis/
QSP/Consultants	*Name:* Compuware.
	Areas of Experience/Expertise: MDA Qualified Service Provider, providing enterprise IT solutions in areas that include IT governance, application development, quality assurance, and application service management.
	Size: More than $2B in yearly revenue, with 7,500 employees worldwide.

(Continued)

TABLE 2.1   Project Profile: Statewide Automated Child Welfare
Information System—Cont'd

	Project Role: Responsible for the development of the system and conversion from the old system.
	URL: www.compuware.com
	Name: Dynamics Research Corporation.
	Size: $300M revenue (2005), 2,000 employees.
	Areas of Experience/Expertise: DRC's primary mission is to deliver solutions and services to U.S. federal, state, and local governments.
	Project Role: Prime contractor for the State of Ohio SACWIS project, with responsibility for overall project management and requirements.
	URL: www.drc.com
Business Pain Points	Federally mandated implementation; 18-month deadline.
	Required support for, and integration of, a patchwork of systems across 88 counties.
	Some previous implementations of SACWIS in other states had encountered serious difficulties, including cost overruns and functionality shortfalls.
Tools Used	Compuware's OptimalJ, Rational Rose, JBuilder.
Model-based Artifacts Created	High-level business models (Rational Rose).
	Platform-Independent Model (OptimalJ "Domain" model) and Platform-Specific Model (OptimalJ "Application" model). The PIM is automatically transformed to a PSM, as mediated by OptimalJ's Technology Patterns.

3

CHAPTER THREE

SOLUTA.NET/ COOPSERVICE CASE STUDY: FACILITIES MANAGEMENT INDUSTRY

An employee-owned company in the facilities management industry uses MDA to implement a governance layer while simultaneously rationalizing its IT infrastructure and supply chain. A business-to-business (B2B) portal and facilities management reference model bring industry leadership in the form of the "integration point" of choice for cooperative projects.

BACKGROUND

Coopservice is an interesting and unusual company. Like many other enterprises in the local region (Emilia Romagna, Italy), it is a "cooperative," meaning that it is owned by its employees, who are called "associates." The mission statement on the Coopservice web page describes its goals in relation to associates rather than customers, and these goals include the improvement of economic, social, and professional conditions; the safeguarding and development of jobs; the involvement and recognition of workers in achieving company goals; and the empowerment of associates in both business and social arenas.

In spite of this internal focus—or perhaps because of it—Coopservice has become a market leader in offering facility management services. Coopservice (see Figure 3.1) has more than 10,000 employees, €374 million in yearly revenue, and €50 million in assets (the official estimated revenue for 2006 is €450 million).

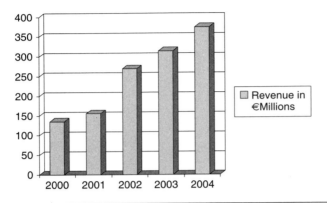

FIGURE 3.1   Coopservice yearly revenue.

Coopservice began in 1991 as the merger of two cooperatives, Cierrepi and Coopsicurezza, whose combined expertise included private security and sanitation. The resulting enterprise has become one of the more dynamic Italian cooperatives, and its fast growth reflects that of the facilities management industry itself.

The cutting edge of the facilities management industry is the provision of services to large enterprises–to deal with cleaning, waste and environmental services, maintenance, building and property management, security, and catering, among other things. A facilities management project is a big undertaking (the typical Coopservice facility management project lasts three or four years, and is valued at about €80 million), and requires the combined efforts of multiple companies to provide the required services.

For example, Italian hospitals often demand a complete packaged solution to their facility management requirements, because of the difficulty and expense of managing the many different individual services (or service providers) required. A hospital needs elementary services such as linen cleaning, building and property management, and security and catering, as well as more sophisticated services such as warehousing and administration. On average, 20 small and medium enterprises and several hundred workers are required to deliver this type of service package.

Large enterprises want "one-stop shopping" for facilities management services

To provide such a package, Coopservice typically outsources many subservices through a network of collaborating enterprises. In other words, Coopservice acts as the prime contractor and coordinates a temporary association of companies for specific customer contracts.

Coopservice wanted to take advantage of technology to improve its business position in the market, and launched the Pant@ project to accomplish this. Its goal was to be able to manage its entire supply chain with a single enterprise architecture that presented two different appearances and sets of capabilities: a custom enterprise resource planning (ERP) application that supports intra-enterprise processes and a B2B capability for connections to other enterprises.

Coopservice wanted supply chain management for its own purposes and a B2B capability to coordinate service delivery with partners

Soluta.net, a Qualified Service Provider (QSP) in OMG's FastStart program, was engaged by Coopservice to drive the Pant@ project. Soluta.net is an international company staffed by senior consultants and architects. It has offered component-based software solutions, consulting services, and technical leadership for distributed enterprise applications since 1994. Soluta.net emphasizes the use of modeling in defining software architectures in order to increase the reuse, and therefore the value, of IT investments. Their expertise spans a number of domains, including telecom, pharmaceuticals, tourism, healthcare, radio communication network infrastructures and terminals, customer relationship management, and enterprise application integration.

WHY COOPSERVICE CHOSE AN MDA APPROACH AND WHAT THEY HOPED TO ACHIEVE

Coopservice was not aware of MDA when the decision was originally made to undertake the project–but they were certainly aware of the difficulties of realizing a project of this size using traditional development tools and methodologies. So, when Soluta.net described the MDA approach in a short nontechnical presentation that described the enterprise-level advantages of MDA Coopservice quickly grasped its significance. They decided to use MDA, and they agreed to undertake a quick proof-of-concept (POC) using Soluta.net's open-source tool JunoMDA. Because the potential benefits were so great, they also increased funding for the effort. When we asked Walter Siri, Project Manager at Coopservice, why they chose an MDA approach and what they hoped to achieve by that choice, he said:

> The main reason we chose an MDA approach for Coopservice was the ability to model the business–for example, business processes–in a way that did not depend on the technology platform or computing techniques.

And when we asked about the business driver behind this choice, he said:

> As a company, we offer service solutions in the areas of cleaning, security, and industrial processes. The delivery of these solutions requires the cooperation of other companies. MDA allowed us to change our approach to the realization and delivery of the solution, to the economic benefit of our customers. We need to be able to dynamically change the process by which we connect with our partners, and in order to do that we need a software development and deployment approach that allows us to respond much more quickly.

The result was the Pant@ project.

CHALLENGES

The Pant@ project had to overcome many interrelated challenges: functional, organizational, technical, and process related. On the B2B infrastructure side, there was a dual goal of automating the transfer of delivery, scheduling, and activity report information to and from partners and creating an inter-business electronic community for the exchange of goods and services.

The goal of the ERP effort was to integrate and streamline all legacy applications such that the application functions would be available to business process workflows. In other words, Coopservice wanted each business process to be a single automated flow that could traverse internal business units and applications. In addition, Coopservice saw the need for a governance layer on top of ERP functions to enable better monitoring and control over the entire firm.

A technical challenge was presented by the fact that Coopservice's existing IT infrastructure consisted of 45 unrelated applications spread across five major lines of business (LOBs), where each LOB had to support approximately 40 primary use cases. Further, these applications used different implementation technologies: IBM AS400, Microsoft .Net, and Java EJB. So, the technical goals of the project included reimplementation on a single architectural style (SOA implemented via EJBs and web services) and the eventual retirement of the legacy systems.

The existing infrastructure contained 45 nonintegrated applications on three different implementation technologies

The final challenge was related to Coopservice's belief that their business models and business processes are strategic assets and competitive advantages. Therefore, they wanted to retain tight control over them rather than sharing control and visibility with suppliers and software vendors.

Business models and business processes as strategic assets and competitive advantages

Coopservice felt it had to maintain control over specification of the architecture and business process customization, as well as over project management and coordination. Architectural leadership was provided by Dr. Pierfranco Ferronato, Chief Architect of Soluta.net, together with Roberto DalleMura of AIM Consulting—but the larger question became, "How do we coordinate and harmonize the many software vendors and integrators needed for this project?" Although acknowledging that the challenges were formidable Pierfranco pointed out one very significant advantage in tackling this project.

> For the first time in my career I encountered a customer who said he preferred to build things better rather than just quicker. I was amazed.

EXPANDING GOALS

Over the course of the project, goals and expectations changed—especially for the B2B and business process aspects as Coopservice became familiar with MDA. At the start of the Pant@ project the goals were "merely" to rationalize existing applications and integrate the supply chain to make it easier for partners to participate in large-facilities management projects.

However, Coopservice soon realized the value of creating a B2B community of facilities management companies, including providers, suppliers, and partners. Through the use of MDA, Coopservice saw an opportunity to provide a common functional reference model for facilities management that would enable partners and enterprises to quickly join together in response to the needs of large customers.

A common reference model for facilities management is a business advantage in an environment of "coopetition"

To be able to cooperate with each other in this way, partners need an IT system built to support this goal. Before the Pant@ project, the only way IT support could be provided for such a multipartner effort was for all partners to use the IT system of the "lead" (prime contractor) company.

For prime contractors, this resulted in a patchwork of adapters and inconsistent data formats from their subcontractors. Subcontractors had to deal with a different IT system for each of their prime contractors.

Coopservice has also embraced the concept of "coopetition"–that is, cooperating with industry players in some cases while competing with them in others. We asked Project Manager Walter Siri of Coopservice how the new B2B capabilities would provide a business advantage in an environment of coopetition. He answered this way:

> We pursue service contracts with enterprises on a competitive basis. But we offer services from a network of companies, and these companies collaborate to fulfill those service contracts. The B2B capability makes it easier for us to define and deliver that solution because it works with all the IT systems that individual cooperating companies use. These cooperating partners find it easier to work with us than with competing "prime contractors," and that is a business advantage for us.

In order to succeed with a coopetition strategy, Coopservice wanted to provide a new–and open–IT system for facilities management. And rather than selling this product/technology, Coopservice wants to maintain industry leadership by becoming the "integration point of choice" for cooperative projects. By 2007, Coopservice expects that their B2B system will provide an open environment for negotiations among industry players, including competitors. In the long term, Coopservice hopes that this effort will be embraced by the International Facility Management Association (http://www.ifma.org/).

Coopservice is increasing its business agility and leveling the playing field for small- and medium-sized enterprises

The plan is for Coopservice to "level the playing field" for small and medium-size enterprises that cooperate to fulfill large contracts. They plan to do this by providing a common functional reference model for facilities management. Because this reference model embodies the formal specification of functional requirements, the coordination and provision of services become much easier to manage and the organization for managing it can be set up much more quickly.

In addition, many of Coopservice's partners are also cooperatives, and providing assistance to other cooperatives is an important goal. But even partners with more typical organizations can realize the benefits of sharing the same open IT support system for facilities management. If a partner does not have an IT support system, they will be able to use the IT framework of Coopservice's B2B portal.

The facilities management industry is growing fast in terms of overall market size, number of players, and size of projects. Coopservice has come to understand that they must exploit cutting-edge technology to take advantage of these trends. And the MDA expertise that Coopservice developed over the course of the project resulted in the expansion of another goal, that of providing the system with a "governance layer." As Pierfranco Ferronato put it:

> The implementation of a governance layer was always a main goal of the project. However, there were many other challenges we had to face before addressing that one, and we thought that we would not be able implement a governance layer until late in 2006. But after four or five months of experience with MDA tools and model-driven development processes we found that it was much easier to do the governance layer than we thought it would be.
>
> A part of this governance layer is already in place. We have implemented a "governance cockpit" that allows real-time monitoring of business processes, and also provides controls for modifying these processes, even if they span lines of business within Coopservice. If properly modeled, these process modifications do not require coding, deployment, or system updates. Thus, at Coopservice governance is not simply portfolio management, it is business process management.

A governance layer that supports business process management

HOW MDA WAS USED

The Soluta.net/Coopservice collaboration began with POC and pilot projects before the Pant@ project itself was launched, although the Pant@ project certainly built upon these preliminary efforts. The POC project used Soluta.net's JunoMDA open-source product to create a web-based demonstration application in a few days. Coopservice was impressed with the results and decided to perform another development iteration—the pilot project—that would further explore MDA capabilities and create usable components for the eventual Coopservice system.

After delivery of the POC, the team spent a short time identifying and defining the set of business-support components to be created in the pilot project. They identified those components that would be most useful to Coopservice as typical and widely used functions and features. Most of these components involved the integration of legacy systems to support the provision and consumption of information across general interfaces that could be used by the pilot components as well as the not-yet-defined components in the eventual system.

The goal of the pilot project was to create enough of a system to allow Coopservice to carry out some part of its business using the components and their associated user interface. The pilot components contained enough business logic to demonstrate the ability to manage and modify business processes at runtime through the use of a control console.

"Tender management" pilots the governance layer

Interestingly, the most important component of the pilot was "tender management"–the first piece of the governance layer. Tender management is the handling of bids to perform a service at a specified cost or rate. The component implemented the business process by which Coopservice received and examined tenders of service. It allowed them to determine which tenders required a response, and it applied the relevant business rules that govern the response. This was a workflow implementation based on the very complex business processes involved in responding to a tender. The complexity came in part because the tender response might cut across various business functions, including security, facilities, cleaning, food services, and so on.

Other, less complex, components were delivered during the pilot project as well. All in all, the pilot resulted in the creation of half a dozen enterprise business components over a four-month period. All were based on computation-independent models (CIMs) and Platform-Independent Models (PIMs). The pilot demonstrated the ability to create a functional MDA-based project, and the decision was made to proceed with the additional development iterations encompassed by the Pant@ project.

PROCESS AND TOOLS

As mentioned previously, Soluta.net's open-source MDA tool was used to develop the POC demonstration project. The pilot project, and the Pant@ project itself, relied on Finantix Studio–a transformative MDA tool that operates within the Eclipse development environment. Finantix Studio was supplied by Finantix. Finantix, like Soluta.net, is a QSP within OMG's MDA FastStart program.

Finantix Studio is used to model the application as well as business processes

Finantix Studio is called a transformative MDA tool because it allows an application to be modeled once and then transformed to target implementations on various architectures (e.g., three-tiered browser-friendly architectures, three-tiered architectures enhanced by a portal server, or rich client architectures).

An application modeled in this way accommodates business-level organizational boundaries in the implementation of business functions, and it clearly separates the specification of business functions from technical concerns. In this way, the intellectual property inherent in the definition of a business function is kept wholly in a PIM.

Further, Finantix Studio allows business functionality to be fully reusable across multiple technology platforms. For example, if a data item is limited in length this limit is propagated to generated code for data input (e.g., Javascripts), network service interfaces (e.g., web services), and data output (e.g., an RDBMS). Thus, reusability applies not only to business logic but to presentation logic, displayed data, persisted data, configuration parameters, and external transactions.

In addition, the tool allows the team to specify business logic via a domain-specific language (DSL), including the modeling of business processes (specifically using Business Process Modeling Notation [BPMN] and XML Process Definition Language [XPDL]). Any business component implemented with Finantix Studio is based on a PIM that specifies the function of the component. The PIM is transformed to a PSM (Platform-Specific Model) by the Finantix Studio transformation engine, and this transformation can be optionally enriched by model annotations specified in the DSL.

The DSL implemented by Finantix supports sophisticated concepts such as persistence, integration, transactions, security, data constraints, configuration, and workflow. The workflow-oriented constructs were particularly useful in the Pant@ project's efforts to formalize and manage their business processes.

DIVISION OF LABOR

When a consulting company undertakes a project with a client, and that project uses a technology or approach new to the end user, there are often two goals. The first is ensuring that the project succeeds, by putting in place people with the right skills. The second is ensuring that the client organization gains enough knowledge and experience to become self-sufficient going forward.

Soluta.net integrated their own skilled consultants with client personnel at all levels in the project while AIM Consulting provided a technical architect, Roberto DalleMura, to work with the project manager and to be responsible for the technical infrastructure as well as legacy integration (such as integration with existing Coopservice security systems). Typically, Soluta.net personnel undertook leadership of the analysis and process activity because they had much more experience in thinking in terms of methodology and enterprise architecture. The actual makeup of the Pant@ project team, and the duration of team positions, was as follows.

- One project architect (provided by Soluta.net): 6 months
- One technical architect (provided by AIM Consulting): 12 months
- One functional architect (provided by Soluta.net): 12 months
- Three business analysts (provided by Coopservice): 15 months
- Four MDA developers (provided jointly): 14 months
- Two or three business analysts to customize models for web services and EJB component-based development (provided jointly): 6 months

An integrated project team tackles legacy integration, process automation, and B2B support

The first phase of the Pant@ project was aimed at improving enterprise resource planning capabilities within Coopservice, primarily by integrating existing legacy applications. This phase was expected to take a total of 18 months, including two months for the first development iteration after MDA was introduced to the organization.

The second phase was aimed at automating internal/private Coopservice business processes. In this phase, business models—including associated services and use cases—are created using BPMN, with the goal of providing application support for these private processes. The second phase began in October of 2005 and is expected to end in Q2 2006.

The third phase is aimed at providing intra-enterprise support, including creation of a B2B portal. Another deliverable of this phase is a Facility Management Reference model, which will provide the basis for a common IT infrastructure for the management of multi-company facilities management solutions. The third phase is ongoing at the time of writing and is not expected to end before the end of 2006.

Functional teams for project coordination, CIM analysis, PIM design, and PIM development

Four "functional teams" make up the overall Pant@ project team.

- The Project Coordination team took the project strategy as input. Its iteration-driven output took several forms: a roadmap, functional domain analyses (such an analysis is a component model, a related set of system-level components consisting of business, entity, and process components), component specifications, and a "feature catalog" that specified required capabilities in the system to be built. This output was in the form of Microsoft Word documents, Excel spreadsheets, and UML diagrams created with NoMagic's MagicDraw. These deliverables together controlled the strategy plan.

- The CIM Analysis team took as input information about Coopservice functional domains, required business components (as well as their respective software life cycles), and a component model for external and legacy systems. The output from this team is driven by use cases, and includes formal use case models, prototypes, and component models for external and legacy systems. The mechanisms for generating this output include UML 2.0 and MagicDraw. In this way, the CIM Analysis team controls the functional architecture, component-based development targets, and model-driven conceptual framework for the project.

- The PIM Design team was responsible for CIM-to-PIM mapping. This team took the use case models, prototypes, and external/legacy component models produced by the CIM Analysis team and produced finer-grained use cases, component and interface specifications, and an integration strategy. Through MagicDraw-generated UML models, the PIM Design team controlled the technical architecture, the migration plan, and the downstream aspects of the model-driven conceptual framework. The UML models included sequence diagrams, class diagrams for persistent and

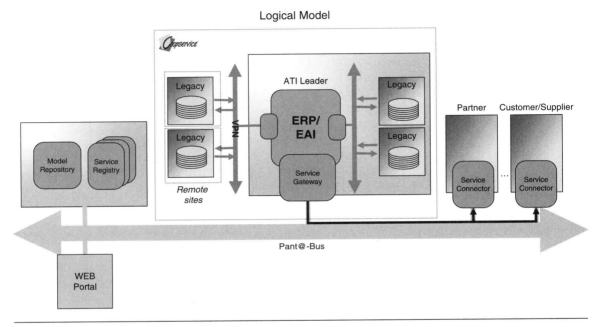

FIGURE 3.2 Pant@project logical model.

transient business modeling, and implementation diagrams for component specifications (which describe ports, required interfaces, middleware per port, and dependencies).
- The PIM Development team took as input the integration strategy, the fine-grain use cases, and the component and interface UML models produced by the PIM Design team. Using the FSX component-based development conceptual framework and the DSL of Finantix Studio, this team produced executable use cases that were run in the test environment.

Figure 3.2 illustrates the logical model of the system to be built.
Figure 3.3 illustrates the technical architecture developed for the Pant@ project.

PROJECT EXPERIENCE

MDA proponents claim that it can improve the communication between an organization's business and IT communities. Pierfranco Ferronato agreed that MDA helped improve such communication in this case but pointed out that you still

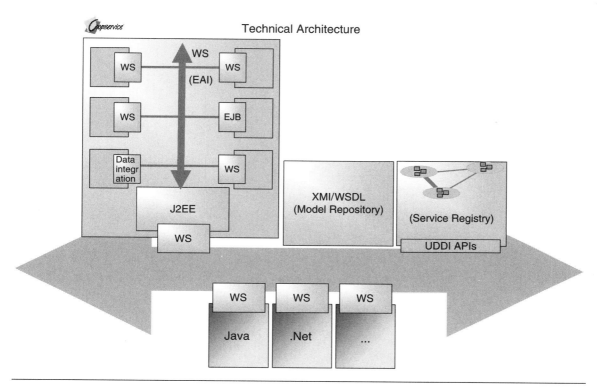

FIGURE 3.3 Pant@ technical architecture.

have to be careful about drawing the boundaries between what is of interest to business people versus technical people.

> We talked with the business community about dependencies between components, functional features (essentially use cases), business object models, business processes, business events, and so on. But we did not discuss computation-specific issues such as interfaces or exceptions.

Thus, the first step of the project was the creation of a CIM or domain model, which captured the desired behavior of the business. Figure 3.4 shows a small portion of the CIM.

The PIM was independent of any MDA tool, which mitigated the risk of tool-related problems

In the next step, the PIM was developed using Finantix Studio. The Studio tool uses the Eclipse Modeling Framework (EMF) as an MDA repository, and it can import and export models. While the language used to create this model was Finantix specific, the PIM itself was independent of Finantix and in fact independent of any specific MDA tool. This fact guarded against any failure caused

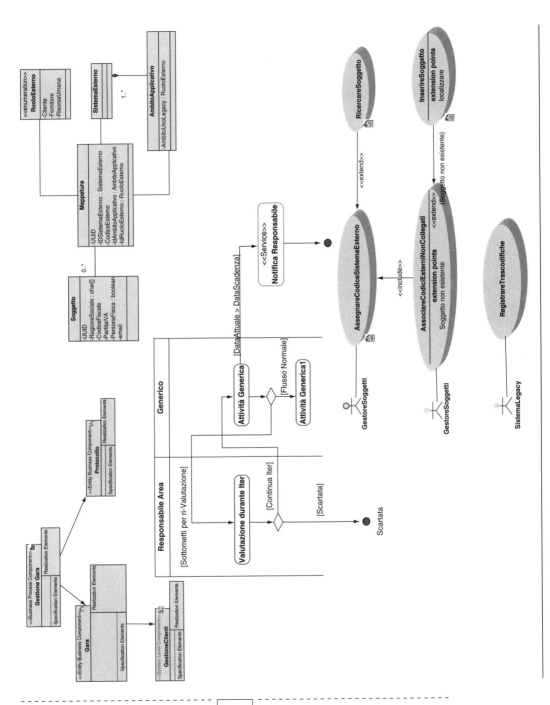

FIGURE 3.4 CIM sample.

by potential issues with Finantix Studio because it allowed replacement of Finantix Studio with some other tool, if necessary, through the import/export of models expressed via XMI (XML Metadata Interchange). The PIM captured 90% of the application semantics (the other 10% being information about data migration and legacy integration). Figure 3.5 illustrates a small portion of the PIM, and Figure 3.6 illustrates the respective content of CIM, PIM, and PSM.

Business analysts were not expected to learn UML or tool usage, but were able to define and manage business processes

We asked whether Coopservice personnel were required to learn UML (or at least a subset of UML stereotypes for modeling elements specific to their business) versus using only the DSL of the Finantix tool. The answer was that in general business analysts were not expected to be able use the Finantix tool itself. Although the tool exposes some UML semantics (including class diagrams, component dependency diagrams, business classes, and state diagrams for use case collaboration), users can specify behavior either by creating a graphical diagram or by using a textual language. The Finantix tool maintains semantic synchronization between the diagram and the textual language.

When a user interaction is defined in Finantix DSL, a state diagram is generated, as shown in Figure 3.7. The state diagram is related to events, and the interaction it specifies executes in the context of a single user session. But business analysts are not expected to manage artifacts such as a state diagram because it is a relatively simple piece of a more complex business process.

Instead, the business users wanted to be able to define the management process for an entire business process (in the same way they defined the tender management process in the pilot) rather than becoming involved in how the user interacts with the application. Thus, business analysts use the Finantix business process console to manage an entire business process (see Figure 3.8). Once the technical team had captured and developed a sufficient set of fine-grain user interactions, the business analysts could use the business process console to quickly adapt the business process to various purposes and to change the logical workflows.

MDA does aid communication, but bridging the business/IT gap is a difficult problem

Pierfranco had more to say about the ability of MDA to bridge the gap between the business and technology communities and the inherent difficulty of the problem.

UML profiles help in keeping technical details out of the PIM

The CIM specification is actually just a "concept" in the OMG specification, and moving from the CIM to the PIM is not an easy task. MDA itself says very little about this transformation, and we had some difficulty in bridging the two models.

Of course, there are obvious advantages to this separation. We are able to create specifications that capture requirements in a form that is understandable by less-technical stakeholders; for example, the project manager. These people were not comfortable with the PIM, but were perfectly able to understand the CIM.

However, the transformation from CIM to PIM requires a lot of energy, and we at Soluta were creating approaches to address this aspect of the project. In the creation of the PIM, we needed to identify and precisely define interfaces: how many interfaces for each component, signatures for methods, ports and responsibilities for

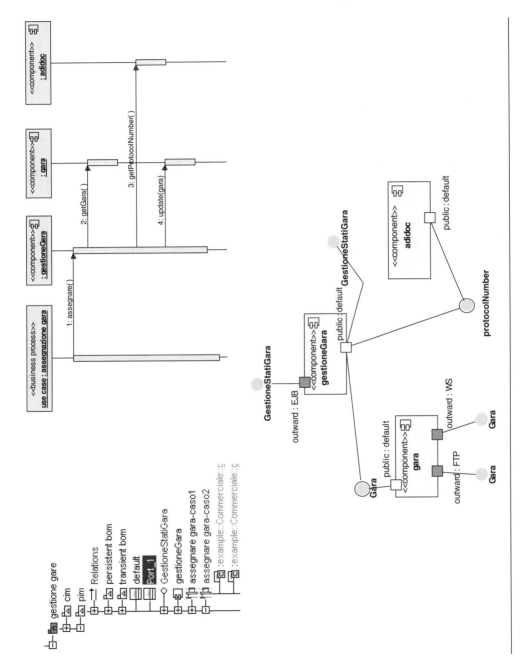

FIGURE 3.5 PIM sample.

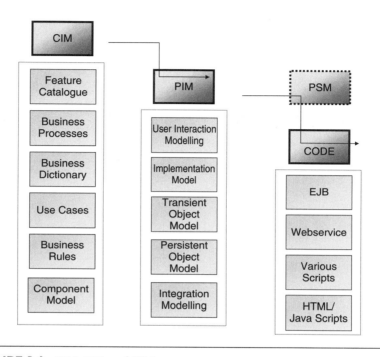

FIGURE 3.6   CIM, PIM, and PSM content.

components. And we needed to decide which responsibilities–which services–need to be exposed externally (outside the company) and internally. We were trying to discern patterns.

For each of these patterns, we might provide a use case, business classes, dependencies, cardinalities, and operations. These responsibilities must be captured from the outside. So, we had to figure out how to use profiles, and how to use UML to describe CIM model elements that are close to the PIM, without specifying all the details required in the PIM.

You need to organize the CIM in such a way that the process of transforming it to a PIM becomes clearer. In some cases, it is difficult to decide whether something should be specified in the CIM versus the PIM, and by extension where this thing should appear within the software factory.

A CIM analyst may have to decide how a legacy system provides requested data in order to fulfill a business requirement. And the question becomes whether to specify the provision of this information in the CIM or the PIM. If it is in the PIM, what is the best representation? A stereotype? A use case? An operation? An interface? If we decide, for example, to use a stereotype for a use case representing an API or a service that is invoked by an external system we need to map this into a technology.

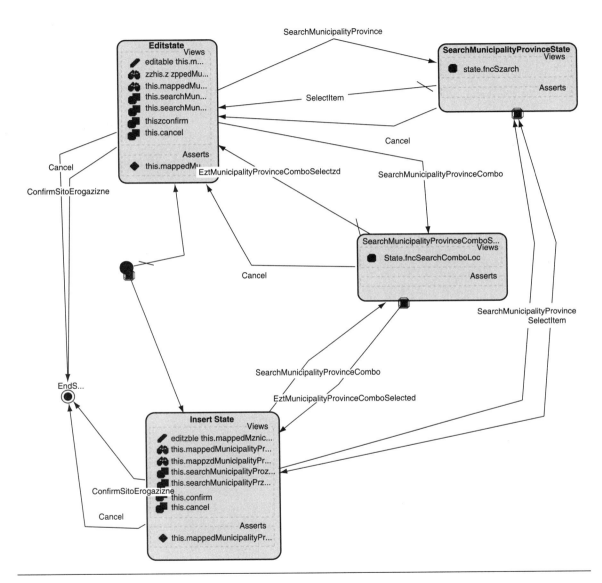

FIGURE 3.7 Finantix Studio state diagram.

One problem is that at this time the transformation of CIM to PIM is not well supported by MDA tools. Not every MDA project begins with a CIM, but those that do may find that the CIM can become disconnected from the software life cycle of the overall MDA project. Essentially, this happens because even CIM models that

Other UML extension mechanisms aid in mapping from CIM and PIM to PSM

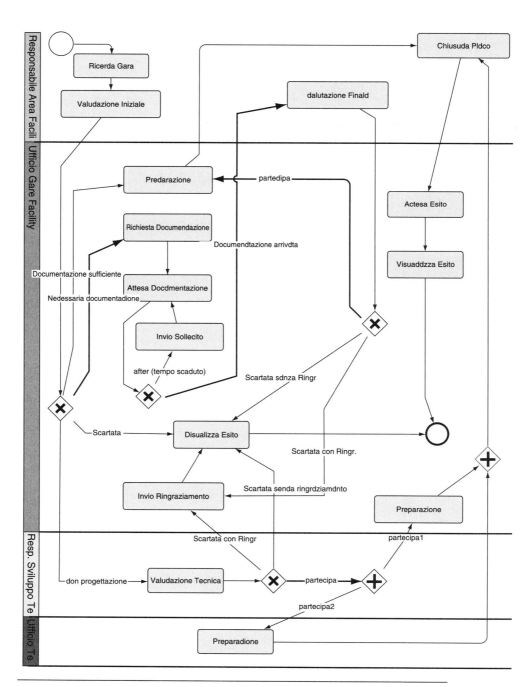

FIGURE 3.8 Finantix Studio business process model.

are precise and complete are not necessarily directly computable. So, this breach in the CIM-to-PIM transformation must be bridged manually.

It takes considerable time and effort to manually trace back and forth between PIM and CIM model elements. Those who need to do CIM/PIM mapping must decide which kinds of UML models to use for CIM modeling because that choice will affect the amount of effort needed to perform the mapping.

Pierfranco also felt strongly that CIM analysis is becoming more and more important. In the past, developers could fix analysis errors "on the fly" because analysis was simply a way to nail down requirements in the form of a wish list whereas functional errors were detected and addressed during coding.

In contrast, Soluta.net and the Pant@ project have developed a team philosophy and culture that says that the CIM is the application, while the PIM is its projection in concrete IT artifacts. Coopservice now has one person in charge of maintaining the template of patterns, which people can refer to in order to understand how to transform one aspect of a business process from the CIM to the PIM. And they are trying to keep the CIM and PIM metamodels aligned enough such that the energy required to transform a model element from the CIM to the PIM is minimized.

The CIM is the application; the PIM is its projection in terms of IT artifacts

Before the start of the Pant@ project, Coopservice had a panel of business experts whose job was to capture business processes. Coopservice was one of the relatively few companies that had developed a set of full, rich business processes. These business processes had been captured/specified using Visio and placed on an internal web site that was not part of the IT organization.

The project team was able to use these defined business processes to great advantage in the Pant@ project, even though there was no connection between these process definitions and IT infrastructure. These were abstract or theoretical process definitions, and people simply knew that certain process steps required various applications as well as manual steps such as phone calls and faxes. However, a significant part of the project's business analysis was based on this work. The Pant@ project took responsibility for all business process definitions, and for making such definitions formal and rigorous.

Abstract "paper" process definitions were made rigorous and formal

Currently, there is an external company that conducts interviews to capture such business information–from sources throughout Coopservice, not just IT. Their output consists of drawings of business processes, which are then implemented and maintained by IT. The project was also very fortunate to have the Pant@ Project Manager Walter Siri as a source of business information. His years of experience at Coopservice meant that he knew the business inside and out, and he was instrumental in the process of cross-checking and validating business information.

In researching this book, the authors often asked questions about "Aha! moments" experienced by the end-user organization–in other words, about events

"Aha!" moments

that caused end users to understand an important benefit of MDA they had not realized before. For the Pant@ project, two such examples were provided.

One had to do with the first time the team provided features in the testing environment. The network manager had been very concerned about the usage of the HTTP protocol encoding. Two people worked for a couple of weeks to address the network manager's requirements in the matter, and were able to fulfill the requirements without changing a single line of functional code. The network manager was very much impressed.

The second "Aha! moment" had to do with the first time the team modified a process using the BPM console. They were able to dynamically change a threshold condition to say, in effect, "If the project is under €100,000, we are not interested in it." People working on the application were amazed that the application's behavior could be changed on the fly in that way.

ORGANIZATIONAL DEVELOPMENT

Although organizational change was not a goal of the original project, exposure to the MDA development process resulted in a significantly changed organization. This is a common occurrence in MDA projects, and Soluta.net had informed Coopservice that such changes were likely.

In the past, Coopservice employed only a very small IT staff for infrastructure maintenance. They did not have an internal team dedicated to software development and instead outsourced most of that function. But because of their desire to maintain strategic control over their architecture, the IT organization had to change to match its new responsibilities.

MDA changes both organizational structure and responsibilities associated with job function

For example, there was a need to employ new types of analysts. Most IT organizations still have the classic "analyst/developer," and Coopservice was no exception. Coopservice COBOL analysts/developers had a good understanding of the business but they had to learn how to maintain the code in an MDA-based system.

An MDA project requires analysts who can provide computable UML models, rather than just functional documentation. And as yet there are not many pure MDA developers available for hire. The project addressed these issues in two ways: through bottom-up training of classical developers to become MDA developers and through top-down training of classical analysts to be MDA analysts. So, the Pant@ project created the organization shown in Figure 3.9.

The Coopservice IT team has been completely restructured as a result of the Pant@ project, and its structure borrows heavily from the Pant@ project's organization. Coopservice IT now has a software factory consisting of three teams: a CIM team, a PIM team, and testers (plus a small team for maintenance). The people in

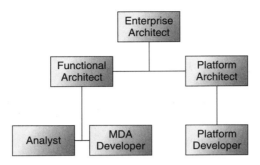

FIGURE 3.9   Project team organization.

these groups are more focused and organized than before. Whereas the previous organization was almost completely flat, there is much more specialization in the new organization. The structure and operation of the software factory is illustrated in Figure 3.10.

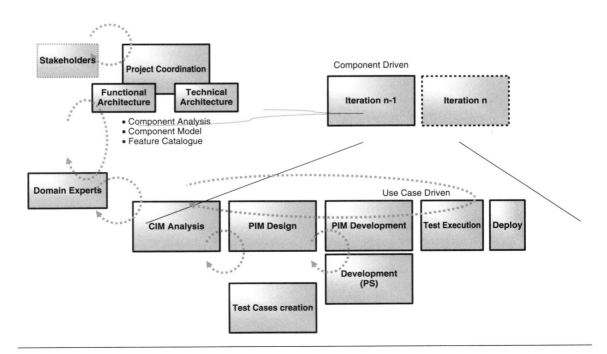

FIGURE 3.10   Software factory process.

RESULTS AND BENEFITS

The PIM proves to be a valuable and reusable strategic asset

One of the major software life-cycle benefits realized by the Pant@ project was the reuse of the PIM across architectural styles. The first release used the default architectural style of Finantix Studio, whereas a customized architectural style was applied to the second release. This had the immediate benefit of allowing the client to avoid complex and error-prone re-factoring of code, and it proved that the PIM was a valuable and reusable strategic asset. In essence, the PSM and its custom architectural style became additional strategic assets whose cost was essentially zero.

In addition, the fact that the MDA approach decoupled the functional and technical specifications of the system lessened the impact of IT turnover, as well as making it much easier to adapt the system to future technology platforms. For instance, the functionality that has already been developed benefited from the introduction of the Rich Internet Application (RIA) based on AJAX. There was no cost for functional re-factoring because it required only a new generation cartridge provided by the tool vendor. We asked Walter Siri to give a specific example of the business benefits of the Pant@ project. He described the use of Coopservice's new governance capability.

Business process automation improves accuracy, agility, and understanding

The best example has to do with tender management or tender negotiation. When we begin to assemble the partners who deliver services within a large enterprise contract, we post public tenders, to which our partners respond. These tenders might be created by the Italian government, for example, or a large hospital, and they describe the business parameters that determine a response. Once a partner responds to a tender, Coopservice needs to decide which business unit is responsible for this tender, and whether or not to continue the negotiation. This internal business process is quite complex, and the automation of this process was included in the first release of the governance layer.

Now that Coopservice has automated the negotiation and management of these tenders, the business process executes much more quickly. Face-to-face meetings are no longer required, and supplementary documentation about the service requirements can be provided to partners automatically. So, the process is both much faster and much less prone to errors. And the business console lets us look at the process itself and quickly understand whether it can be improved.

It was not unusual for companies in this industry to have defined their own tender management process. But before this capability was provided to Coopservice its process was described by way of PowerPoint slides. So, although this process was well defined it was not automated or even connected to IT systems.

It was also difficult and time consuming to modify this process. Now this process can be modified to support a particular partner very quickly—in seconds. And the commercial process (that of signing service delivery contracts with partners) has been separated from the process of managing these relationships.

The business advantage of this capability is significant. Fewer resources are needed to carry out the process, and it all happens much more quickly. Where it typically used to take a week to reach agreement on a tender it now takes only two days. This is extremely important because tender offers have a deadline, and if Coopservice does not respond in time the tender lapses.

In addition, the time saved in responding to a tender can be used to manage the tender and the relationship with the partner. Coopservice has a large network of partners in the delivery of their enterprise service solutions, but the key capability in assembling these multipartner solutions—and winning the enterprise business—is the ability to respond quickly to tenders from those partners.

This tender management capability has only recently gone into production, so hard statistics on the business improvements are not yet available, but the most recent release has allowed Coopservice to respond to all tenders that have been offered. In the past, the slowness of the process typically resulted in failure to respond to 30% of tenders.

The Pant@ project is ongoing, but the results so far have demonstrated significant improvements over traditional software development approaches. The team estimated that over three years the analysis phase took only 20% more time than typically required in the classical development process. But on the development side they achieved a reduction of more than 80% in the time spent in platform-specific coding—essentially because the MDA tool was already providing a great part of the required PIM-to-PSM transformations.

Overall, the team estimated that the project would have taken 16.5 labor-years of traditional software development. The project in fact required only 7.5 labor-years (once MDA processes and tools were in place), resulting in a total reduction of 53% and an estimated saving of 28% in elapsed time (the team estimated that they could achieve a further 40% reduction in elapsed time in future projects now that they are proficient in MDA techniques). Over three years, the estimated total savings in cost was approximately €510.000.

CLIENT ASSESSMENT OF THE MDA EXPERIENCE

Walter Siri was quite clear about what he originally found intriguing about MDA: the separation of concerns (i.e., the ability to model and examine the business separately from the technical details of the supporting system or its development platform). What he found most impressive about MDA was that it actually delivered on this promise. When we asked how MDA changed the thinking patterns and behavior in the company and its employees, he said:

MDA did not change the business vision of the company. But it does allow us to fulfill our business requirements much faster and more efficiently than before.

We then asked, "If someone in a position like yours said they were thinking of starting an MDA-based project, what advice would you give them?" His answer was:

I would tell this person to first make an assessment of tools used in the company, as well as IT assets such as legacy systems, and to track down the dependencies between these systems. Then, try to optimize the integration of these applications in order to improve business response time. MDA lets you think in terms of the business viewpoint rather than the technology viewpoint, and you should take the business viewpoint.

Walter Siri has a good sense of humor, too. When we asked, "If a nontechnical person asked you what MDA is how would you answer?", he said:

It is something that can allow you to do business without falling into a trench–or at least warn you that you are about to fall into a trench.

TABLE 3.1   Project Profile: Coopservice Pant@ Project

Company/Organization	*Name:* Coopservice.
	Industry: Facilities management.
	Size: €450M (estimated 2006 revenue).
	Geographical reach/extent: Italy.
	URL: www.coopservice.it
QSP	*Name:* Soluta.net.
	Areas of experience/expertise: MDA Qualified Service Provider, emphasizing the use of modeling in defining software architectures; provider of component-based software solutions, consulting services, and technical leadership for distributed enterprise applications.
Business Pain Points	Dual goal of automating the transfer of delivery, scheduling, and activity report information to and from partners, and of creating inter-business electronic community for the exchange of goods and services.

(Continued)

TABLE 3.1   Project Profile: Coopservice Pant@ Project—Cont'd

	Existing IT infrastructure consisted of 45 unrelated applications spread across 5 major lines of business, with each LOB supporting approximately 40 primary use cases.
	Applications used different implementation technologies: IBM AS400, Microsoft .Net, and Java EJB.
	Need to retain control over business models and business processes as strategic assets and competitive advantages.
Tools Used	JunoMDA (open source). Finantix Studio.
Model-based Artifacts Created	CIM. PIM. PSM (code). Business process models.

4

CHAPTER FOUR
SELECT BUSINESS SOLUTIONS/AUSTRIAN HEALTH AUTHORITY

An Austrian government social services agency incorporates MDA into its software development process in order to integrate the IT infrastructure of its distributed suborganizations and to standardize and enforce its technical architecture.

BACKGROUND

The Austrian Health Authority (Hauptverband) is the central organization of the public social security (Soziale Sicherheit) organizations of Austria. Such public companies are effectively government agencies that serve the good of the country, much like the National Health Authority in the UK or the Social Security Administration in the United States.

Austria has a population of about 8 million people and a size of about 84,000 square kilometers, so their healthcare infrastructure is widely distributed, as are the supporting information systems. The Hauptverband provides services in the areas of methods, tools, and infrastructure to the 20+ members of the Austrian Healthcare Association.

Select Business Solutions (SBS) is a leading international software company with customers drawn from the Global 1000. SBS provides comprehensive solutions consisting of pragmatic tools and services for business-critical IT software development, deployment, management, information access, and enterprise reporting. Headquartered in Boulder, Colorado, SBS operates sales offices throughout North America and Europe in addition to a network of international distributors.

The project to be undertaken by the Austrian Health Authority was called Zentrale Partner Verwaltung (central partner administration) and involved the creation of a web-based system to manage information about all of the parties with which the organization does business, including doctors, employers, and insured parties. The project itself required the cooperation of suppliers, contractors, and internal teams from the various healthcare association suborganizations.

Hauptverband wanted to move its central infrastructure toward the Java/J2EE platform, and to use a rigorous Java software development process that would allow them to work more effectively with their internal teams, as well as with outsourced suppliers and contractors. They want to standardize an architecture and a development approach across the organization.

Hauptverband wanted a more rigorous development process and a standardized approach to architecture

In the past, projects were based on a custom methodology, which originated more than 10 years ago and has been adapted to specific projects from time to time. Hauptverband was looking to incorporate new and more productive ways of doing things. You could say that they are simply a forward-looking organization that wants to use modern technology to better accomplish their goals.

They are trying to integrate the old with the new, and therefore they want to leverage legacy systems. They needed to create an architecture that integrates those legacy systems in a more flexible and agile way and therefore wanted to do things such as "wrapping" legacy applications to provide service-based access to legacy functions.

In essence, they are creating a scalable architecture that allows new technologies to coexist with old and that provides a clear path on which to move forward. They chose the Zentrale Partner Verwaltung (ZPV) project to test the SBS MDA approach to see whether that would help them achieve these goals.

WHY HAUPTVERBAND CHOSE AN MDA APPROACH AND WHAT THEY HOPED TO ACHIEVE

Hauptverband's selection of an MDA approach was mainly a side effect of their relationship with SBS. Hauptverband had been using SBS tools for more than a decade. Hauptverband became aware of MDA on their own (that is, apart from their relationship with SBS), and they realized that MDA might provide the type of project methodology they needed to achieve their goals of architectural and development consistency, use of best practices, and high productivity. Due to their long-standing relationship with SBS, Hauptverband engaged SBS in 2000 to help them better understand SBS's MDA product offerings.

In 2004, SBS demonstrated how their approach and tool set could help Hauptverband realize some of their architectural ideals and aspirations. Hauptverband evaluated this proposed MDA solution, as well as SBS's ability to provide

SBS is selected because of their MDA tooling and proven professional services expertise

professional services in support of this project, and chose SBS to help them develop it.

A significant driver of this decision was the ability of SBS's MDA tools (specifically, Select Component Architect) to generate a variety of implementation artifacts from a PSM, and to support Hauptverband's higher-level architectural and organizational goals. Hauptverband wanted to formalize a model-driven approach to software development in order to increase productivity in development activities, to enforce architectural standards and best practices for the J2EE platform, and to increase reuse of artifacts in other projects.

They hoped that the use of UML models that reflect problem and solution domains, and MDA's ability to synchronize these models, would increase their ability to reuse and maintain intellectual property. They also hoped that the use of UML would ensure consistent communication flow between teams.

Finally, they expected that the ability of SBS tools to capture and enforce their architectural, coding, and development process standards would increase conformance across projects. Use of this tooling was also expected to increase productivity in the modeling tasks (and artifact generation) associated with Struts, the open-source Spring Framework, EJBs, and Hibernate data persistency mappings.

The biggest challenges faced by Hauptverband included the heterogeneous IT landscape, and distributed IT management, necessitated by the 20+ suborganizations involved in social security and healthcare activities across Austria. Different mainframes and transaction monitors are used by the various suborganizations, and decisions about IT infrastructure are decentralized.

At this point in some of our case studies, we have described the phenomenon of "expanding goals" as organizations become more familiar with what can be achieved with MDA. And although Hauptverband was pleasantly surprised by the relative ease with which their MDA-based development process could handle changes, and with the productivity increases they realized—both capabilities were beyond their original expectations—their project goals did not expand as a result.

An intense focus on their original business goals, and an almost stealthy approach to the adoption of MDA

All of our case study participants chose MDA for business reasons, and all have been exceedingly pragmatic about the adoption and use of MDA. But Hauptverband's intense focus on achieving their original business goals—they expect the project to deliver a functionally complete high-performance software application on time and at budget—takes this pragmatism to a new level.

Although they were willing to discuss their general hopes and expectations for using MDA in different ways, and in future projects, they simply would not talk about any firm plans in these areas until this project is complete and the actual results are tallied. It is also interesting to note that Hauptverband, like the State of Ohio Job and Family Services organization, took almost a stealthy approach to the introduction of MDA, at least outside the project team itself.

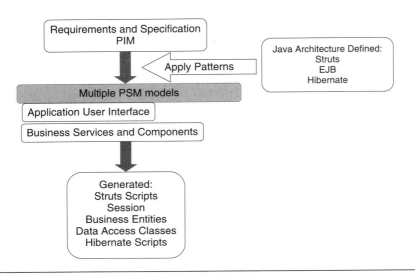

FIGURE 4.1　PSM transformation and artifact generation.

HOW MDA WAS USED

Business and software analysts from both Hauptverband and SBS worked to create a PIM, or logical analysis model, using the SBS Select Component Architect tool. In this case, the Hauptverband personnel on the project team already had considerable previous experience in architecture and UML modeling.

As Figure 4.1 shows, the PIM was transformed to a PSM for the target J2EE platform, and the PSM incorporated the desired architectural patterns so that they could be applied consistently throughout the application. Implementation artifacts (including Java code and Hibernate scripts) were then generated from the PSM.

We asked Barry Maybank, Professional Services Manager at SBS, to confirm that the modeling effort began with a PIM rather than a CIM. His response was:

> No, we did not [create a CIM], and this was purely a matter of pragmatics. We began with the Platform-Independent Model. In fact, they had other models in place from previous work, and some of those models went straight into the PSM. But the work was essentially a matter of doing a PIM and then transforming that logical model into the physical PSM.

Another useful change to the Hauptverband development process was the notion of an iterative/incremental approach. We asked Uta Terlinden, Technical

The modeling effort begins with PIM, not CIM

Manager at SBS, whether modeling helped Hauptverband tighten up their requirements specification. She answered:

> Yes, it did, because the old process they used for gathering requirements (which could be characterized as structured design) is not really suitable for a UML-based project. The changes that we've introduced into the process include the incremental approach, and that helped.

In addition, MDA had an important effect on Hauptverband's technical architecture, which we discovered when we asked about the gathering of requirements and communication between the business and IT communities in light of the fact that the project did not create a CIM as a "pure" business model. Uta answered:

> It is true that no CIM was done. The requirements were gathered using a different SBS product, in the context of a bigger project that was started earlier and was then canceled.
>
> So, the analysis phase for that project was done with a different tool. Later, they began using an MDA approach after a new technical architecture was agreed upon for the entire Hauptverband.
>
> They had an earlier technical architecture, which was quite "heavyweight"–to the extent that it was nearly impossible for specialists to roll out this technical architecture for other projects. Essentially, the architecture had too many degrees of freedom. The MDA approach was appreciated by the customer very much, because they saw it as an opportunity to roll out a new technical architecture–for the first time–to the entire organization.

In response, we suggested that this sounded as though MDA constrained the technical architecture in some way (such that they had more guidance in how they implemented it) and asked Uta to expand on this.

A new technical architecture is rolled out–in which the correct use of patterns is enforced

> Yes, they had started with a PIM and a PSM, and they had a second team that was responsible for implementation of the technical architecture. They were using an Oracle database, Struts, and Hibernate for relational mapping. It wasn't clear how they would deal with the rules for the technical implementation.
>
> There was a team responsible for the core definitions. They had been rolled out and tested during the project, and the technical team was able to enforce the use of the correct technical constructs. This made it much easier to implement the technical architecture.

PROCESS AND TOOLS

The ZPV project began near the end of 2004 with a training session conducted by SBS. The training included a feasibility study and management seminars to explain the potential benefits of MDA. When the decision was made to proceed, SBS began training project practitioners in the course of the project itself.

A one-week workshop introduced the MDA approach to the project team. The aim of this workshop was to present the initial templates for model transformation, and to demonstrate the generation of code. As a training exercise, the group was successfully shown how to further develop templates. In that single week, the group defined the rules for transformation from PIM to PSM, and from PSM to code. For example, during this workshop they developed a template for mapping from activity diagrams to Struts code and interactions. Uta Terlinden of SBS led this workshop and described it in this way:

> They were familiar with UML and had also done Struts projects before, so they were very familiar with the target technical environment. After they understood our approach—our metamodel, which is very important when using Struts—it was very easy for them to write these PIM-to-PSM and PSM-to-code templates.

Uta said that since the workshop, she has visited the site once or twice and has provided some advice by telephone, but "the project now runs by itself." Hauptverband has been using a well-defined methodology since about 1994. This methodology is mandatory and is tailored to their specific needs, and it is now being enhanced with MDA tools and techniques (such as the incremental/iterative approach). We asked Barry Maybank of SBS to characterize Hauptverband's current development methodology. He answered:

"...the project now runs by itself."

> It is definitely an incremental and iterative approach, as are many software development methodologies. The client defines increments as a unit of delivery, and they are seeing that MDA supports this incremental approach. It is not simply about "top-down," it is about both top-down and bottom-up, about defining units of work, and being able to drive transformations based on those units of work.
>
> So, MDA certainly supports this. For example, we were defining details in various artifacts for only a limited scope of the project, as defined by the increments (that is, involving a limited number of use cases).
>
> But the model in its entirety was of course much bigger than that. MDA certainly helped in the handoff of these increments from analyst to designer, and in doing refinements between iterations. This of course fits in with the agile notion of development as well.

At mention of the word *agile* we asked Barry whether he agreed with other case study participants who told us that MDA and MDA tooling fit well with agile methodologies—precisely because the quick generation of tedious and error-prone low-level code allows developers to concentrate on developing business logic and algorithms. He answered:

MDA plus agile software methodologies...

> I would agree with that completely. This customer is working with large teams, and with external contractors. So, although they want to be agile they also want to be

...provide the benefits of agility with better practices and greater control

in control of things. I think the MDA approach satisfies both those objectives. With automated code generation, they can get the right level of control over productivity and best practices—by exploiting MDA's separation of concerns and by applying patterns, which takes them right down to the code level.

That gives them a quick approach to their code base, and of course it can quickly change things in them. The ability to control the transformation of models means that they can control their implementation artifacts. This fits with the level of rigor they want, as well as the agility and productivity they want from an agile approach. So, I think MDA and agile development are complementary rather than in opposition.

I find that some clients have XP-style teams. This works very well for small teams where everyone knows what is happening. Communication is so efficient that things usually work out. But most of our clients realize that this is not always the case. They have much larger teams, distributed teams, and partially outsourced teams. They want to retain the agility benefits but also get greater control and better practices. So, the Austrian Health Service is using benefits of the MDA approach to satisfy all those objectives.

Recall that the purpose of revamping the Hauptverband technical architecture was to help coordinate efforts across all suborganizations of the Austrian Health Authority. The previous standard architecture (although clearly defined) was somewhat outdated, and this became more and more limiting for new projects. Inconsistency in project implementations caused many problems for Hauptverband, which they now believe can be addressed by an MDA approach.

SBS tools specify and enforce architectural patterns and general coding practices, including variants

The SBS tooling lets them specify—and enforce—architectural patterns and coding practices, but the overall process goes beyond implementation of the technical architecture. It also describes the way a project works; for example, by specifying the deliverables and the way in which those deliverables are mapped into the next phase.

The process also supports variants in project deliverables, and these variants can be described precisely in the transformation rules. Thus, Hauptverband has a metamodel of the architecture that is always consistent and that is enforced by the tooling and the related process descriptions.

And if a project needs to do something special, they can simply use the tool to tweak the process in a well-defined way, rather than abandoning the process completely. In this way, they can get the result they need without leaving the overall architectural guidelines.

Figure 4.2 illustrates a sample architectural artifact. Analysts developed these business entities in a PIM, and an MDA transformation generated business entities, interfaces, data access objects, Hibernate mappings, and approximately 50% of the implementation code (including inline comments).

The ZPV project went through project definition, requirements analysis, product design, and product development stages. The functionality was provided

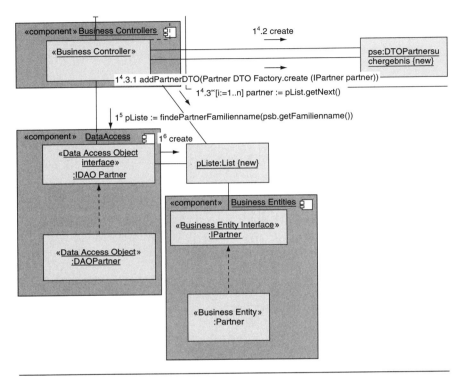

FIGURE 4.2 Sample architecture artifact.

in three incremental releases. The chosen tooling is SBS's Select Component Architect and the Select Solution for MDA Code Generation. Custom scripts are used to generate code as well as other types of implementation artifacts, such as Hibernate relational mapping logic.

DIVISION OF LABOR

The total size of the ZPV project is estimated to be 6,900 labor-days, with incremental deliveries spanning 2005 to 2007 and a team consisting of one project manager, one architect, six analyst/designers, and seven software developers.

At the beginning of the project, a one-day workshop was attended by managers, architects, and analyst/designers. Its purpose was to define the concepts, principles, benefits, and issues that surrounded the adoption of the MDA-based process.

Practitioners are immediately taught to create MDA templates for Java architectural patterns

A three-day workshop was then conducted for all practitioners, to prove the concepts and to teach by example how Java architectural concepts are implemented as MDA templates. Project initiation and rollout activities for SBS tooling took three to five days over a four-week period. The architecture and design and activities included SBS's facilitation of the continuing effort to identify and define MDA pattern templates and transformations, with the goal of ensuring that the new MDA process was "fit for purpose" in implementing the new architecture and process.

This was followed by a one-week period in which SBS coached all participants on the process and identified and fixed any problems discovered in templates and transformations developed to that point. An ongoing activity by architects and process owners is the capture of recommended strategic approaches and solutions, so that Hauptverband can consolidate lessons learned on this project into best practices for the future.

The remarkable thing about the division of labor in this project is the large proportion of work done by Hauptverband. SBS provided initial training about the capabilities, benefits, and use of MDA. Hauptverband then implemented MDA on the project. SBS continues to provide review and guidance on the project, recommending best practice usage of MDA within the project environment and architecture, but as Uta Terlinden said this review and guidance now amounts to an occasional telephone call.

Hauptverband personnel are responsible for more than 80% to 90% of project work

For the workshop and the initial project stages, three people from SBS and 10 people from Hauptverband were involved. In the project itself, there were three people from SBS and 12 people from Hauptverband (including external consultants), plus an additional Hauptverband team of three who were responsible for the technical architecture and for implementation of transformation rules. Lorenz Lercher, Chief Technical Architect at the ZPV Project of the Austrian Health Association, described the division of labor in this way:

> SBS provided significant resources at the beginning of the project, in order to give us a quick start and to bring us up to speed on the use of the tools. After that, we were able to do most things on our own and that is the case today. Overall, I would say that SBS did between ten percent and twenty percent of the work during the start-up phase and introduction of their MDA tooling.

PROJECT EXPERIENCE

As in the case of the Inherit/Harris case study (Chapter Five), this project was not a "pilot" in the traditional sense, because it implements critical functionality for Hauptverband and most of its suborganizations–that of replacing distributed and redundant data stores with a central one, and migrating and unifying business logic on a common platform. But it is a pilot in the sense that the level of success of this project and methodology will drive the application of MDA in future projects. Lorenz Lercher responded in this way to our question about the specific data-related goals of the project:

It is about managing the data. We have high-level services that can be used to access the data, so there is no direct access to the underlying data for other systems. Through those services, the system manages the data to ensure consistency.

The services also embody the business rules, so that by using the services and the existing interfaces data can be entered, used, and managed by all the applications and systems that have already been written.

There are two access modes. We provide real-time access during the day, so that administrators and clerks can ask questions of clients, and get answers from the system and update data, etc. And at night, batch applications run against the data; for example, for mass changes.

We suggested that creating an architecture that allows an application to support both complex batch and online transactions is no small problem, and asked how MDA helped sort out the architectural issues involved. He answered:

MDA clarifies architectural issues related to data access in both real-time and batch modes

The main use of MDA in this area was to ensure that, as far as possible, the same business logic was applied in both kinds of access—for both online access and a batch fetch. The main issue for the batch access is always performance. Still, we tried to have as much business logic in common as possible for both tasks by changing only the technical aspects of the data access; for example, transaction boundaries.

The project is not finished yet, so if it turns out that there are performance problems in batch access we will do performance optimizations for data access and will try not to duplicate logic. We want the same system for batch and online access.

Barry Maybank, Professional Services Manager at SBS, was involved in this interview and added the following observations and question to the discussion.

When I was in Austria with you folks, I was witnessing MDA transformations to create some of the application framework code. And I witnessed some of the EJBs and session beans being generated from a logical model. And then, likewise, in the data access layer using Hibernate, and you were using MDA to transform to Hibernate scripts. Would that be an example of the kind of architectural patterns that were enforced and automated with MDA?

From what I saw, it was a very well-architected system, delivering services to one or more applications and having very well-defined sets of responsibility to solve a complex problem in conjunction with the use of other technologies. And you seemed to use MDA to enforce those architectural principles, as well as providing the glue logic.

Lorenz responded:

MDA relieves developers of the "glue code" chore and reduces duplicate business logic

Yes, that is true. We tried to pull out the business logic and separate business logic issues and technical issues. So, for example, transactions are not part of the business logic proper because in our use cases transactions simply start when the back end is called and stop when the back-end service is finished.

In the user interface, which is a web application, the steps of the business process are managed—all other business logic is called as services from the back end. In batch jobs, the business logic in the back end is reused; only technical aspects like transaction boundaries are different.

The technical architecture we have is very well suited for reuse in combination with MDA. It supports the separation of glue code and business logic. So, generally this is a very important issue for us—on the one hand not having to write the glue code by hand, and on the other hand not having to duplicate logic. Instead, we reuse code automatically thanks to code generation and the use of frameworks like Spring.

We often ask case study participants the very general question of whether MDA improved communication. We asked Lorenz Lercher whether MDA artifacts were exposed to any of the suborganizations that make up the Austrian Health Association, and whether any of those suborganizations were involved in the MDA aspects of the project.

He said that although those suborganizations see specifications from the project, and are kept officially informed of results, this information is limited to prototypes of the application, plus paper reports based on parts of the model and other generated artifacts—much the same kind of information that has been provided them in the past.

We then asked whether MDA made it easier to generate and deliver this information to them, and whether this affected their ability to verify the quality of the implementation. He responded:

> I'm sure that it helped, but I have to say that they had similar information in previous projects before MDA. So MDA is a good way to do this, but there were paper reports before.
>
> We were able to generate that information from the model. We did some customizing of the tool in order to accomplish that, so I think that at least for this project it is easier to get information out in those reports used by this group.

MDA's effect on deployment and maintenance

We also asked Lorenz whether he thought MDA would result in any improvement in the deployment or maintenance characteristics of the new application. He said:

> With respect to maintenance, I think that that is a function of the specific changes that are required over the course of the application's lifetime. MDA is a methodology very well suited to this, because the changes can be specified at a high level, and it is clear how the change will manifest itself in the code.
>
> Most of the coding details are fixed as a result of the business logic being specified. So, for maintenance MDA is a very good thing because the patterns in use are always the same and are used in the same way. So, if you see a pattern in one place you can be sure the pattern is used the same way throughout the application.

Of course, developers have always tried to encourage this kind of uniformity in usage, but in practice there were always slight differences. And this often caused problems. I think this is the greatest MDA advantage in terms of maintenance.

I think deployment is really separate from MDA. It depends on the patterns, in the background, that are used in the architecture. You use MDA to generate new code and if it is a good architecture that makes deployment easier. But this is independent of the technology used to generate for a specific architecture. If the architecture is well designed then deployment will be easier. But in terms of dealing with changes MDA is very important.

RESULTS AND BENEFITS

The results of this project cannot be completely described yet because the project is ongoing. But all concerned are happy with the results so far, which include the following.

- Enforcement of architecture and standards while increasing productivity in both the design and development effort.
- Due to the automation provided by SBS tooling, the overall quality of the development life cycle has improved, resulting in less rework and consequently shorter development cycles.
- Model and implementation are synchronized, which provides much better traceability for considering and measuring the impact of changes.

The project has thus far hit all key development milestones, even those near the beginning of the project (March through April of 2005), where the learning curve of participants had to be accommodated. The model-driven approach has increased quality throughout the life cycle thanks to templates and transformations and has improved the transformation between PIM and PSM, resulting in the automatic generation of more than 50% of the Java implementation code (including inline documentation). Thus, MDA has allowed them to formalize the architecture and automate much of its enforcement.

All key development milestones have been reached on time

Although the benefits of MDA as a communication medium have not yet spread to the business community or to the suborganizations of the Austrian Health Service, the SBS contingent believes that MDA did improve communication between the analysts and designers. As Barry Maybank put it:

> As is the case for many of our clients, some of the straight UML models became too abstract and "too logical" for the designers to find much value in them, or they became "too physical" in nature and therefore became incomprehensible to the analysts.
>
> So, there was a semantic mismatch between these two teams, and that is certainly one of the reasons why Hauptverband felt that MDA was the right approach for

them: the fact that they could (first) separate out those abstractions to the benefit of the longevity of project and solution and (second) express their best practices in terms of architectural design patterns and apply them in the transformation between the PIM and PSM.

So, that was a key driver for them, and I believe they are realizing that benefit. Certainly within the project team that is true.

When we asked Uta Terlinden about the more intangible benefits of MDA in the context of this project, she said:

> The first benefit was better communication between the architecture team and the project team. Before, the project team was not really following the instructions about the technical implementation. In some cases it was because they did not want to follow such strict rules, and in other cases there were simply misunderstandings.
>
> But this project demonstrated clearly how the technical architecture should be used, as well as the mapping between PIM and PSM. That made the technical architecture much more pure.
>
> It also meant that people who were new to the project were able to use these templates to gain a deeper understanding of the technical architecture, and that saved a lot of time. They were able to take part in the project much sooner than originally estimated.

Uta echoed other participants when she said that an important lesson was that generating implementation artifacts from a more abstract business-centric model made it easier to identify and consistently implement architectural patterns that appear many times in the project.

Chances of MDA success are increased in a forward-looking organization

But the successful application of MDA was due in large part to the forward thinkers at Hauptverband. When we asked Uta whether there was an event or episode that made her believe line developers had "gotten it" with respect to MDA she said:

> The fact that they were not in a rush to get to "cutting code" and that they realized that investment in building the MDA templates up front would give them quality and productivity benefits later.

CLIENT ASSESSMENT OF THE MDA EXPERIENCE

As we mentioned previously, the Austrian Health Association's Hauptverband is very conservative in their evaluation of MDA because the project is not yet finished. We also mentioned that Hauptverband, like Ohio's Job and Family Services organization, used what could be described as a "stealth" approach to MDA introduction. Lorenz Lercher, Chief Technical Architect in the ZPV project, mentioned the reason for that stealthy approach in answer to our question about whether there was any resistance to the introduction of MDA techniques.

No, but that was caused in part by the fact that we did not actively promulgate MDA, at least not outside the project. The communications undertaken with people outside the project didn't change. The advantage of not promulgating is that people did not say, "I don't like these changes."

We asked Lorenz whether there was any confusion or learning difficulty within the project. He responded:

Let me think about this. I think it is important that the people who worked on architecture, and were in control of the process, that they have a clear idea of what it means. I did not see more difficulties with this project than with any similar project.

I think the relationship between the different artifacts, at different levels, is clearer with MDA, and the clarity of these relationships may make it easier. So, while there might be some difficulties in terms of where to put information (for example, sometimes there might be too much technical detail at too high a level), this is a problem that we've had in the past, so these are typical problems not MDA problems.

The relationship between the different levels is clearer now, because it is clearly defined in terms of how to transform from one to another. If you do this by hand, it is possible to violate those relationships and cause confusion. So, in this regard it is easier for people to see what belongs in one model versus another, and how these models relate to one another.

The SBS team noted some important points about Hauptverband's adoption of MDA: they used MDA to *improve* their existing development process rather than replace it. And the fact that MDA made that existing process smoother and easier—without introducing a steep learning curve or significant cultural change—simply meant that MDA did not get in the way and that the organization did not need to be overly aware that they were doing an MDA project. When we asked Uta Terlinden, Technical Manager at SBS, about her impression of Hauptverband's awareness and acceptance of MDA she said:

MDA improved the process without a steep learning curve or significant cultural change

The people who are in charge of standardization of processes are certainly aware of MDA. The rest of the company is not really aware of it. They know that there is a pilot project that uses this new process, and that it uses a component architecture and UML tools, but they're not really aware of MDA.

We then asked her whether MDA awareness had reached the programmer level, and if so whether they had any concerns about it. She answered:

Yes, they are aware of it. At first they were a little bit concerned because they had to follow strict rules that were not in place before. But that has changed as they see their productivity and quality improve, and as they find they can spend more

"...within 15 minutes they essentially understood everything..."

time implementing business rules and architecture. But at first they were not really pleased about it, because of employment concerns.

But the people responsible for standardization of transformation rules and code generation are really happy about MDA. The team leader, who was responsible for architecture and process, is really happy with the MDA solution because he can ensure that the rules are followed by these different teams.

The person I spoke with first was the team leader responsible for implementing standards across the organization. He was searching for a way to develop standards and to bring them into the company, and MDA fit perfectly.

When we introduced our MDA approach to the project team, they became convinced that it would help. They had a very short amount of time to implement this project. The project leader was easy to convince.

When I introduced MDA to them, within 15 minutes they essentially understood everything, and were saying things like, "Okay, it looks like this will solve our problems. Let's try it!"

It was unbelievable. Normally, it takes time to convince someone that MDA will help. We met in Vienna with three or four people, and after some conversation it was clear to them within minutes that our solution was a perfect match for their problems. And they had not even seen our tools yet! I have never before seen that happen so fast.

We asked Lorenz Lercher to characterize any differences he saw between their pre-MDA methodology and the current one, and whether he could think of any "Aha!" moments the organization experienced during this project. He replied:

"MDA...just summarizes the longtime experience that many of us have had."

At the moment, MDA is used in the project to make it successful. It was not the first order of business to make MDA more useful in the agency. We just wanted a successful project, and this is a big project for us.

The things we learn during the development of this project will be put into our methodology, and incorporated into our best practices. But at the moment this has not yet been done. So, if we are successful, and I think we will be though we're not yet finished, then MDA will be used to enhance our methodology.

But it was not a goal of the project to adopt MDA throughout the organization. We simply wanted a methodology that would result in a successful project. After that happens, it is almost certain that what we learn will be applied elsewhere.

I am personally very convinced that MDA is a good approach. It just summarizes the longtime experience that many of us have had. It provides a language to express what we have been trying to do all these years.

So, MDA is a very good methodology for projects, to separate business issues from technical issues and to avoid redundancy of logic and associated problems.

I think that this is the way people ought to think about the processes associated with a project. And when you have to produce software artifacts, code generation is very important. Code generation changes how easy it is to make changes. You can change something at a high level in requirements and it propagates down to the code.

The good thing about MDA is that this works very well, because many things can be generated, and it is clear where the requirements came from for generated code. MDA makes you really think about the process of software development and I think that is a good thing.

"MDA makes you really think about the process of software development and I think that is a good thing"

We told Lorenz that we understood his unwillingness to predict future usage of MDA until this project is complete. But we did ask him about his opinions on these matters, based on what he had seen so far, and whether he was hopeful that they would succeed and that they would be able to reuse what has been learned on other projects. He replied:

Yes, surely. I'm sure that MDA was good for this project and that we will reuse what we have done here with this methodology. I think we will try to integrate what we have learned in our own in-house process, which we have been developing for about 10 years now. We need to capture these things and write them down so that everyone does things the same way. But I'm sure we will use these things in our next project.

We asked Lorenz two final questions. The first was what his advice would be to someone who said they were considering an MDA project. He said:

I would say to them that MDA is certainly a good idea. The thinking behind it is very good. Because it is widely used in different projects, I would encourage them to use MDA.

And I would always say that you have to pay attention to the tools. They will have to use new tools. Whenever you change methodologies or technologies, you will have to learn new details about using tools. I would congratulate them on deciding to use MDA because I am really convinced that this is the way to do enterprise-level development projects.

"I am really convinced that this is the way to do enterprise level development projects"

The second question was, if a nontechnical person asked you "What is MDA?", what would you tell them?

I haven't thought about this much. But I would probably say it is something like having a map of the world, or of a country, with multiple levels so you can zoom in to see more details. And so you have two or three levels of maps, and MDA is about the relationship between the overall map, and then painting in the details as you move down the levels.

TABLE 4.1   Project   Profile: Austrian   Health   Authority   Central   Partner Adminstration Project

Company/Organization	*Name:* Austrian Health Authority (Hauptverband).
	Industry/function: Central organization of the public "social security" (Soziale Sicherheit) suborganizations of Austria.
	Size: Support for Austria's "social security" agencies, covering a population of more than 8 million people across 84,000 square kilometers.
	Geographical reach/extent: Austria.
	URL: n/a.
QSP	*Name:* Select Business Solutions.
	Areas of experience/expertise: MDA Qualified Service Provider, supplying comprehensive solutions for business-critical IT software development, deployment, management, information access, and enterprise reporting.
	URL: *www.selectbs.com*
Business Pain Points	The need to move to Hauptverband's central IT infrastructure toward the Java/J2EE platform, and to use a rigorous Java software development.
	The desire to standardize on an architecture and a development approach across the organization and its suborganizations.
	The need for an architecture that integrates legacy systems in a flexible and agile way, allowing service-based access to legacy functions.
	The need for a scalable architecture that allows new technologies to coexist with old, and that provides a clear path upon which to move forward.
Tools Used	SBS Select Component Architect.
Model-based Artifacts Created	PIM.
	PSM.

5

CHAPTER FIVE

INHERIT/HARRIS CASE STUDY: TELECOMMUNICATIONS INDUSTRY

A telecom/IT company uses MDA to improve and speed up the process by which its product can be tailored to the needs of individual customers. It plans to provide its downstream customers with both the models and the know-how to tailor the application to fit their own requirements.

BACKGROUND

Harris Corporation is an international communications and IT company, serving government and commercial markets in more than 150 countries. Headquartered in Melbourne, Florida, Harris has annual sales of $3 billion and employs more than 13,400 worldwide, including 5,500 engineers and scientists.

Harris provides "assured communications" and information technology to government and commercial customers, with an emphasis on high levels of performance and reliability. Harris views its ability to innovate, integrate, and manage advanced communication technology on behalf of customers as a key competitive advantage.

Inherit, LLC, is an IT consulting firm that concentrates on empowering organizations in the adoption of MDA. This focus makes use of their considerable expertise in project management, development methodology, and software architecture. Inherit is an MDA Qualified Service Provider and offers a suite of consulting services, including a rapid systems development approach for both custom-built applications and the integration of existing systems, to create enterprise solutions.

Harris wanted to change an existing telecommunications management application into one that could be tailored easily to meet the specific needs of various customers. This effort became known as the Managed Telecom Service Enterprise (MTSE) project and was funded from the Research and Development budget.

Harris knew that they had a lot of work to do, and were facing schedule pressures. They recognized that they needed external assistance and decided to outsource part of the project to help them stay on track. They looked for a company that could support their IT needs and help them create a high-quality business solution efficiently—that is, in a way that maximized the productivity of Harris IT staff.

Harris has a very sophisticated software development organization. Their software process conforms to the concepts of CMMI (Capability Maturity Model Integration), and they have the discipline to follow the process faithfully. The Harris team contains very good architects, engineers, and developers and they have a great deal of experience in doing large-scale projects.

This broad experience prepared Harris to engage in MDA-based software development—although they were perhaps not considering it for this project. They did not demand MDA expertise of the vendors who competed for the outsourcing contract. And Inherit, which won the business, did not market itself as an MDA shop. However, Inherit had been developing its own MDA-based approach for some time.

During the course of the project, a joint team of Harris and Inherit personnel captured requirements in the form of use case diagrams and detailed use cases. These use case artifacts were then used to develop additional UML models: class models, sequence diagrams, and state diagrams. The analysis of these requirements drove the creation of a PIM (Platform-Independent Model), which was then used in tandem with transformation rules to create the PSM (Platform-Specific Model). The transformation rules enforced conformance to Harris coding standards and guidelines, which ensured a smooth integration of the target architecture with Harris's existing system.

The PIM was modified over several iterations and was then used to drive the development of the PSM, which was in turn utilized to generate the code/text model. The working application generated from the code model allowed the business community to determine whether the requirements were valid, and whether they had in fact been met. After each review, the PIM was modified accordingly and the process was repeated.

The result was the development of a successful application that was delivered on time and under budget. This success is in turn encouraging the adoption of MDA-based software development into other parts of Harris Corporation.

Note that the illustrations in this case study are general depictions of a PIM, a PSM, and sample output of the transformation from a PSM to text. Because of the sensitive nature of the Harris application and its use in classified environments,

Harris needed to make its telecom management application more easily customizable, while maximizing the productivity of their IT staff

Harris and Inherit captured requirements in UML models, analyzed these requirements to create a PIM, and then created a PSM customized to support Harris's architecture and software development guidelines

Harris understandably declined to provide any specific descriptions of the application or its architecture.

WHY HARRIS CHOSE AN MDA APPROACH AND WHAT THEY HOPED TO ACHIEVE

Harris felt that the tailorable telecommunications management application they wanted to create was more a business challenge than a technical or IT challenge. Like many enterprises, Harris has its own guidelines for software development and architecture. The architecture they had in place was based on core J2EE design patterns that supported the use of EJBs for the application server, Struts for the web presentation layer, and Oracle and Microsoft SQL for the persistence.

Harris required that the new application conform to this architecture, but they also wanted to be able to support deployment of the application in different ways. Target deployments included an application service provider (ASP) model (whereby they would host the application for customers) as well as a "black box" (or turnkey) model, whereby the entire solution would be delivered to a client.

Harris asked several software vendors to consider providing a solution. Each vendor spent a day with Harris. In the morning, Harris described the problem they wanted solved, and in the afternoon the vendor described what their approach would be in creating a solution.

Inherit is a small company, and was competing with some very large vendors. Some of these companies had already provided software to Harris, and so these large vendors were the software "incumbents."

Inherit presented MDA concepts and tooling, winning the business from much larger–and incumbent–software competitors

When it was Inherit's turn, in the second half of the day they presented the MDA concepts of PIMs, PSMs, and so on and then used their MDA Express tool to demonstrate the generation of code. At that point, Harris saw that the Inherit approach could solve the immediate problem–that of very quickly creating a tailorable telecommunications management application. Harris also noted that the MDA approach could give them a strategic competitive advantage going forward, by giving their downstream customers the ability to use MDA artifacts and techniques to tailor the application themselves.

The ability to help and support downstream customers in this way was particularly important, because the Harris business unit responsible for the MTSE application views other Harris divisions as customers and as channels for this product. This was the point at which Harris began to notice the broader business value of MDA.

Inherit was not competing against other MDA vendors, and MDA per se was neither an issue for Harris nor part of their design for this system. Yet, when Inherit showed MDA to Harris Inherit won the contract. Harris recognized the potential benefits in applying MDA to their product stream, and that in order to achieve the described MDA benefits they would have to become self-sufficient in this technology. In fact, part of the contract negotiation was an arrangement for Harris to license Inherit's MDA Express tool, which is not generally available for purchase.

But it bears repeating that Inherit was brought in on the basis of a pure business decision: Harris decided that Inherit could save them money by helping them develop their target system quickly. Harris was looking for a partner that had experience with requirements gathering, modeling, and telecommunications. Inherit made it to the bidders list because of their experience with telecommunications and UML.

Rob Mitchell, principal and cofounder of Inherit, believes that what ultimately closed the deal for them was the demonstration of their internal MDA Express tool. During their afternoon presentation they used the tool to build a UML model, and from that model they built a PIM, generated a PSM from that PIM, and generated code from that PSM. Their generated code could be deployed seamlessly into the application server Harris had chosen. And this prototype code was based on Struts and EJBs, which was the target application environment Harris had chosen.

David Almeida of Harris had the role of program manager of the MTSE project. When Almeida saw the MDA capabilities, he quickly realized they would help productivity for this particular solution. But he also saw that his team and his organization could incorporate MDA into their software development process—and that they could use that capability to do just what Inherit was doing, which is winning business by differentiating themselves from their competition.

Harris knew that they were going to build a solution to be sold to various clients and that each client would require some level of customization, which Harris had expected to have to do by hand. David Almeida realized that Harris could build a core application with MDA to show to customers. Harris could then tailor the models to reflect each customer's needs and then generate a substantial part of the custom application. They saw that as a significant competitive advantage.

We asked David Almeida specifically whether he anticipated the benefit of applying MDA techniques for future business opportunities, in addition to those that were on the table at the time. He said:

> For sure. As a program manager, one of the things I look for is risk mitigation. I saw a "big picture" in which MDA, and in particular our experience with Inherit, as being a great risk mitigator for programs that have large software content.
>
> Our vision was based on the 80/20 "Pareto principle." If I could get them to produce 80 percent of the low-level code—kind of the horsepower under the hood—while I spend my effort, time, and resources focused on the domain of the application (that is, specifying the requirements the application must meet to satisfy my customers) then so much the better.
>
> And I think that any program manager in the world who has budget and time constraints, and is looking for ways to mitigate risk, can use MDA as a method that allows them to identify and stay focused on that 20 percent of capabilities that really satisfy their customers' requirements.

MDA brought mitigation of project risk, and the ability to focus more on customer requirements than on technical requirements

The themes of risk management and increased focus on end-user requirements came up repeatedly in our conversations with David, although risk management was the concern that originally drove the choice of Inherit as a project partner. As he put it:

> Our challenge was driven by schedule. There were some opportunities that we were pursuing, so it was a time-to-market issue. From a program management perspective, when you are looking at budget and schedule issues and so on, one of the key things that we were constrained to do was to achieve a production-quality capability in a very short period of time.
>
> We held a bidder's conference and brought several vendors in. Most of those who came in and presented were traditional "body shop" types. The most innovative thing we saw was the Inherit MDA Express solution, because they not only brought some domain expertise in telecommunications but they also, and in my mind more importantly, brought a toolset that would allow us to achieve a high quantity of code and a repeatable method (which also speaks to some level of quality), and they were able to do that in a short period of time.
>
> So, we issued them a subcontract [...] and we issued a tightly defined scope of task orders. Our challenge was to produce as much high-quality code in as short amount of time as possible, while meeting our budget constraints. That pretty much sums it up.

Rob Mitchell of Inherit described the winning of the contract in this way:

> Harris was considering bringing in other solution providers, and each of them was given a full day with Harris. Their intention was to keep their reactions to these presentations close and guarded, so that they wouldn't give away their thoughts on how different presenters were doing.
>
> But when we showed them how a well-structured, well-formulated MDA tool could satisfy their needs we saw that they were very impressed with the capability. The tone of the conversation shifted from "Why should we think you guys are qualified to solve this problem for us?" to "How could we use this tool on other projects?," "How can we incorporate this capability into our products?," and "What kind of business relationship would we have to have in order to use your MDA approach and your suite of tools in other projects?"
>
> Part of the contract that we ended up signing with them included their use and acquisition of the tool, and how they can then go forward with this MDA capability within their organization.

CHALLENGES

Harris knew from the beginning that the most significant challenge facing the MTSE project was schedule, but the size of that challenge became more apparent over time. As David Almeida said:

I think that as we started really digging into the system engineering requirements and fleshing out the software requirements that came out of that, and then analyzing the derived requirements, we all realized that there were a lot more requirements that had to be matched than there were hours available in our schedules to achieve them.

We pointed out that although there are many program managers who face schedule pressures relatively few have chosen MDA as a way of reducing development time. And we asked David what predisposed him to address the schedule challenge in this way. He said:

> On this assignment, our biggest risk was schedule. I don't want to seem arrogant, but I am fairly progressive when it comes to introducing new technology to solve hard problems. That is the intent of technology and the value that it brings.
>
> So, as we asked questions of Inherit, and as we drilled down into how they go about doing what they do, and how MDA helps (as well as their past performance in several other projects in which their tool had been used), my analysis was this: We have a huge risk on the schedule side. I see a tool that can really help me compress that schedule, and I see mitigation points all along the schedule. One of the key things we did to mitigate our risk was to incorporate Inherit into our team. So, we actually had the Inherit people sitting in on our design reviews, our requirement reviews, and in some cases leading portions of those reviews and discussions.
>
> And having said all that, if a program manager can size up a budget/schedule constraint in particular, and if they can get an understanding of how this technology can serve them, it becomes a fairly easy or benign trade-off. And that is how I approached it. When I talk to some of the program management people back in the Harris Government Division, that is pretty much how I describe it to them.

Inherit is invited to attend-and in some cases lead-design and requirement reviews

We then asked David whether previous experience in the use of modeling technology made him more inclined to accept MDA. His answer included an interesting point–that the decision to use MDA could be validated quickly.

> There was one particular program on which we did some modeling, but I think the decision was mostly driven by their [Inherit's] presentation. We were well prepared in our bidder's conference, asking certain questions and so on, but my thought was "I will know within six or eight weeks what my results will be," so it wasn't the kind of thing where you need two years to figure out whether it was the right decision. So, the short answer is, yes, I have been exposed to modeling, but that was certainly not the driving factor behind my choosing MDA as a solution.

EXPANDING GOALS

Harris's initial expectations were heightened by the demonstration of Inherit's MDA tool, but at that time they had not been exposed to the MDA approach to building an application. After engaging Inherit, Harris's initial expectation was that Inherit would simply gather some requirements and then generate an application. Inherit would deliver the generated code and work with Harris to extend that code as necessary, and that would be the end of it.

Business requirements were captured in UML models, and technical requirements were captured in a Struts/EJB "Archetype"

But something different happened. First, there were two tracks of requirements gathering. The first track was requirements that were specific to the business and what the business wanted to implement. The second track was technical requirements, which addressed the architecture of the software solution Harris wanted to deliver. So, while one Inherit consultant was capturing requirements by way of use cases and UML models a second was gathering technical requirements.

To address the technical requirements, Inherit modified the set of mappings, tables, and rules within the MDA Express tool—which together drive the transformation from PIM to the desired PSM and in turn from PSM to the target code and supporting files. Inherit refers to this set of transformation mappings as an "Archetype." In this case, the starting point was the MDA Express Struts/EJB Archetype, which was modified to make its output precisely fit Harris's architecture and coding guidelines.

Second, there was more than one iteration of the business requirements process. Because of the MDA Express tool's ability to capture requirements quickly, it was possible to generate prototypes of increasing complexity that demonstrated implementation of the requirements captured to that point.

Going through multiple iterations allowed Harris to inspect each iteration, make comments, modify business requirements, include anything that had been overlooked, and identify areas into which they wanted to extend the model. These things resulted in modifications to the models and were expressed in subsequent iterations.

In the end, Inherit delivered significantly more than Harris expected, both on the business requirements side and its associated models, as well as in the ability to align the generated code with Harris's method and style of building software. Further, the code was in general bug free (at least, after unit testing, Harris did not report any bugs to Inherit). This was accomplished by "meta-debugging"; that is, the modification of the Struts/EJB Archetype in a way that ensured the generated code conformed to Harris's architectural/design patterns and coding guidelines.

In other words, all bugs of this kind had been cleaned up in the models themselves, which resulted in delivery of code that was bug free. So, there was no extra cost in delivering the software, and the project stayed within budget constraints and came in ahead of schedule.

HOW MDA WAS USED

As a starting point, Inherit took Harris's existing business requirements and produced a PIM. The Harris PIM consisted of class models as well as activity, state, and sequence diagrams. In addition, Inherit iteratively extended the business requirements with use cases that in turn drove the creation, updating, and refinement of the PIM. When asked how Inherit applied MDA to Harris's problem, Robert Lario replied:

> For us, MDA is about two concepts: models and transformations between models. In the same manner that people build models of their requirements and translate those models into design models and finally into text models, we use Inherit MDA Express.
>
> Together with Harris we built UML models and utilized Inherit MDA Express to apply a library of transformations that we call an Archetype. We have an out-of-the-box Archetype called Struts/EJB which captures all the transformations for generating a PSM from a PIM and text models from the PSM to create a solution based on Struts and J2EE.
>
> Our existing Archetype served as the foundation for the transformations, but as part of the engagement we had to modify some of the rules and templates in order to align the generated code with Harris coding standards as well as their existing code. What's interesting about this process is that in parallel the archetype modifications had is own iterative software life cycle of gathering requirements, design, implementation, and test. [See Figure 5.1.]

The project was not a pilot in the traditional sense, because the code and other artifacts produced had to support a well-established product. The team was expected to create production-quality code that was to be integrated with applications Harris already had—and of course the project had to satisfy a direct business need.

The MTSE project was to produce production-quality code while "piloting" the MDA process

But from the standpoint of adopting an MDA process and mind-set, this project could be considered a pilot. It allowed Harris to understand the concepts of MDA, to get some experience with MDA tools, and to see how to incorporate MDA into their existing software development process.

We always ask case study participants whether the use of MDA improved communication between the client's business and IT communities. Robert Lario, principal and cofounder of Inherit, answered that question this way:

> Yes, definitely. The MDA approach we used helped improve communication and understanding between the business and IT communities in several ways. We captured requirements with use cases. We built a PIM that was separate from any implementation details. And, we focused on business entities and their relationships in the PIM which gave the team a good perspective of the business aspects of the application.
>
> But there was also the fact we were able to take use cases and using our MDA Express tool quickly generate working software that they could use to validate the accuracy of the requirements. So, they could see these models in what could be described as executable form and very quickly correct them.
>
> I think the combination of use cases, the UML models that were built from them, and then the software that was quickly generated significantly increased the

Code generation results in much faster validation of requirements by the business community

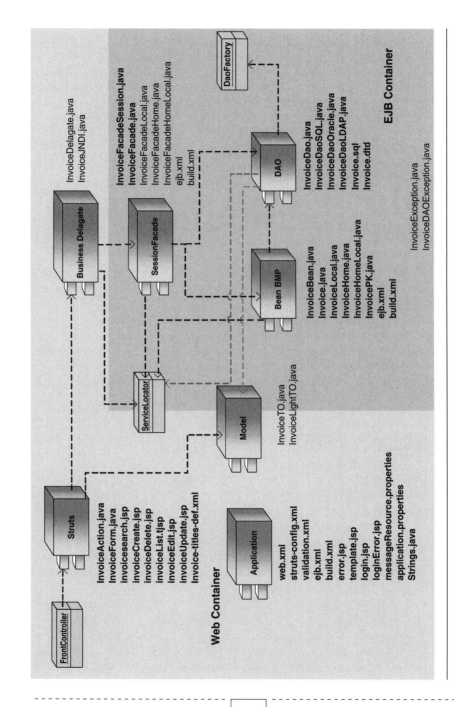

FIGURE 5.1 Sample output of the application of the Struts/EJB Archetype to PSM.

understanding of business requirements throughout the team and provided a way to capture those requirements and increase the quality of the resulting code.

There is also an interesting effect, in that the business people were able to be part of the process in a new way. They were used to gathering requirements, but in this case they were also brought in and shown what those requirements, in tandem with the Struts/EJB Archetype, produced. This helped garner support for the solution that was finally delivered.

The business people were intimately involved and had a feedback mechanism as we built the models during the various iterations. That improved communication with the business community and it meant that they knew what they were getting before it was delivered. They were ready for it and already happy with what they were going to get.

The fast feedback loop improved communications and meant "no surprises" in the deliverables

There was another, and less expected, dividend from the MDA experience, and that was improved communication between the Harris software engineers and system engineers who participated. David Almeida emphasized that the new process used to capture requirements, as well as the ability to generate low-level code very quickly, raised the level of discussion such that more time and attention was given to that of user/usability requirements and less time was spent on the technical details of how the system was implemented. David said that as a result the specification was much closer to what was actually desired, because it was derived from a discussion of what users needed.

MDA improved communication among the software engineering, system engineering, and business communities

PROCESS AND TOOLS

There was little need for negotiation between Inherit and Harris on the topic of software development methodology. Inherit strongly suggested use cases, and defined for Harris the concept of developing a PIM, then the PSM, and using MDA tooling to generate code—in what is essentially a use-case-centric approach.

Harris expected this approach and was happy with it. In addition, Harris viewed the project as a mentoring activity in which Inherit personnel joined their team, walked them through the steps, and developed the product in conjunction with their own people.

So, Inherit provided on-the-job training by jointly going through iterations of the process with the Harris team. No specific training courses were given, but Inherit would occasionally devote a few hours to training about specific concepts so that the combined team could move forward with those ideas. On the topic of software methodology in general, and the process chosen for this project in particular, Robert Lario of Inherit said:

We were an integrated team. It was not as though we did some work and the client's personnel did other work, and certainly not that we did all the work. It

Inherit and Harris become an integrated team

was a collaborative effort and it definitely involved hands-on mentoring about the process.

We support a variety of software development methodologies. We try to support the needs of all our clients, and will work within their process whether it is a waterfall process, the unified process, agile development, or some other iterative process. We have skilled consultants who are familiar with all those processes.

When we have the opportunity to introduce our own process, or define a new process for a client, we use a unified process—something that is use-case driven, architecture centric, incremental, and iterative. We generally focus on the high-risk stuff first, which falls in line with the unified process, but those are the aspects of the iterative process that we like to emphasize.

More recently we have been working with some of our clients in the use of an agile MDA approach, and we've had some good success. We find that our tools and experience fit well with such newer forms of the development process. So, we would like to think that we have married the MDA process with agile software development. In short, we empower our clients with MDA.

The MTSE project combined MDA with agile software development

The difference between software development processes for commercial versus government-specified systems

We asked David Almeida to compare Harris's software development organization and process approach to that of his experience in other software organizations. His answer reflected some of the basic differences in approach between the creation of commercial software and that of government-specified systems.

I have worked mostly in commercial organizations, and the difference is that typically government customers have a set of requirements that essentially demand a more mature process. So, the thing that I appreciate about what we've done in the government division is that we are still commercially viable (our stock has hit an all-time high, with significant gains over the past four years), but having been exposed to SEI and achieved CMM Level 3, and are currently going through CMMI certification, which is integrated CMM. I think that the reviews, the documentation requirements, the demands of our "command media" (that is, our policies and procedures) really add rigor to our analysis in software development.

And look at what our software programs are doing! For the FAA, we are managing their national network that runs the operational data for the national airspace. We are working with other programs to do information retrieval and analysis. Harris has a legacy of solving really hard problems, and this particular software organization happens to follow a very mature process.

The process for this project first dealt with business requirements. Inherit began by generating use case diagrams and developing a supporting use case survey, which encompassed all of the different use cases and actors. Once those were complete (and once the technical requirements had been addressed as described previously), customer-specified modifications were made to the PIM and these modifications were built into all of the artifacts created in the subsequent transformations. These artifacts included deployment descriptors, Java code, XML files,

Struts, EJBs, Struts descriptor and configuration files, tile files, database schemas, and an Ant command file to build the JAR and EAR files.

Four tools were used in this software development process. Rational Rose was used to capture the PIM, as illustrated in Figure 5.2. Inherit's MDA Express tool was used to create the PSM as well as code/text files (by way of XMI import/export, as described in material following), and Gentleware's Poseidon for UML was used to contain the imported PSM generated. The fourth tool was Harris's chosen IDE.

A mixed bag of tools were needed to address Harris's chosen software development approach

Inherit MDA Express combines a web service interface and a variety of plug-ins that enable third-party UML tools to communicate with this web service. The plug-ins are customized to work with various UML tool vendors (e.g., System Architect and Poseidon). As long as a third-party UML tool exposes an API and is XMI compliant, the Inherit MDA express engine can work with it. The tool/process works as follows.

1. Using a third-party UML tool, a PIM is built.
2. When the PIM is ready to be converted into the PSM, the Transform to PSM menu item is selected as well as the desired transformation. Inherit uses the term *Archetype* (which is a collection of patterns/templates and transformation rules that govern the model-to-model transformation) to categorize the offered transformations. In this case, Struts/EJB was chosen.
3. The PIM captured within the third-party UML tool is converted into XMI and the MDA Express Web service is called. This invocation passes the model document and the name of the selected Archetype to the web service.

Platform Independent Model (PIM)

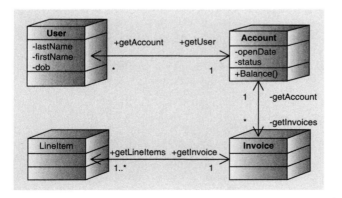

- Domain Business Model
- High Level of Abstraction
- Technology Neutral
- Can be reused
- Contains Business Requirements

FIGURE 5.2 Platform-Independent Model.

4. The web service reconstructs the XMI representation of the UML model into a metadata repository (MDR), which is an in-memory UML model. The tool can support several methods of representing the rules for transformation, including JESS (*http:/herzberg.ca.sandia.gov/jess/*) and iLog jRules. For the Harris project, the iLog jRules engine was used.

5. The transformation rules are loaded and the expert system runs against the in-memory UML PIM model. This model represents the patterns/ specifications of the PIM, and the transformation rules use these to assert new facts about the UML model. These new facts are incorporated back into the MDR, thereby extending the PIM and creating the PSM (as shown in Figure 5.3). At the end of this process, the engine converts the in-memory model back to XMI and returns the document to the plug-in.

6. The plug-in loads the XMI back into the third-party UML tool. The newly generated PSM can now be displayed and modified as necessary within the tool's UML environment.

7. When the PSM is ready to be translated into the code/text model, the Transform to Text menu item is selected. The model is converted into XMI and the web service is called again.

8. The XMI representation of the PSM is loaded into the MDR and the rules engine runs against the model to create the supporting text-based artifacts (Java code, scripts, XML, JSP, C#, C, C++, deployment descriptors, project files, and so on) for the selected Archetype. The Archetype selected is the same transformation that was originally used to transform the PIM to the PSM.

9. When the process is complete, all of the created artifacts are placed in a Zip file (persevering directory structure) and the entire Zip file is returned to the plug-in. The plug-in can be configured to unzip the file into a project directory (Eclipse, NetBeans, Microsoft Visual Studio, and so on), from which the project file can subsequently be opened by the supporting IDE.

The reason for doing it in this way was that Inherit had built a new transformation engine for MDA Express, and this engine did not support the then-current plug-in for Rational Rose. But the team wanted to take advantage of that new engine because it had important new declarative capabilities that provided much more flexibility in customizing transformations.

The code generation step created the project file. When the team opened the project file in the NetBeans environment, all of the code and other artifacts were integrated with the IDE. It looked as though the project had been built specifically for NetBeans.

The target architecture was three-tiered, with JSPs deployed on the web server and EJBs deployed to the application server. Although the production database

Platform-Specific Model (PSM)

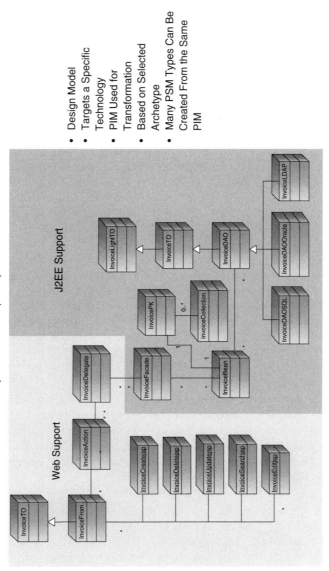

- Design Model
- Targets a Specific Technology
- PIM Used for Transformation
- Based on Selected Archetype
- Many PSM Types Can Be Created From the Same PIM

FIGURE 5.3 Platform-Specific Model.

A database access design pattern supports testing in both normal and secure environments

was in Oracle, Inherit generated Java code as well as both Oracle and Microsoft SQL scripts.

The Java code and SQL scripts allowed the Inherit team to test on machines in an unclassified environment, while the Oracle-specific Java code was used for testing in the classified environment. This flexibility in the generated code was made possible thanks to the use of the bridge design pattern, which allowed the team to change the configuration files for the factory in which the database access layer was specified. This design allowed Harris personnel (who had the required security clearances) to easily take over the classified testing function.

DIVISION OF LABOR

The amount of effort contributed by Harris and Inherit over the course of the project is described in the material following. But the real story here is not about the division of labor at all but about the creation of an integrated team. However, it is interesting to note that Inherit personnel provided only three labor-months of effort during the course of the entire project.

Harris provided three senior systems engineers, who were focused on the business layer, to determine how this technology should be applied across a particular market space. Two of these systems engineers were responsible for defining the systems engineering technical requirements. Inherit personnel translated some of these systems engineering requirements into software requirements, which involved fleshing out the use case model and building the actual UML model.

Finally, Harris provided one software/applications engineer who worked on the user interface Inherit was developing. The applications engineer took the application from Inherit, moved it to the application environment, ran tests, and then migrated the application into Harris's virtual production area. David Almeida described the value of being able to consider the business aspects of making the technology available to an entire market rather than focusing more narrowly on the business aspects of a single system.

> This particular R&D effort was not targeted at a specific program but rather at a capability to address a broad market. Because of that, we ended up taking more than the average amount of time in requirements gathering.
>
> I believe we looked at a dozen different program specifications, in order to gain a firm understanding of their respective business cases, so that we could define the business layer and then translate those into generic requirements.
>
> We probably spent even more time on this because it had sort of a "build it and they will come" orientation to it, rather than that of a program specification that is funded by a particular customer. So, we looked at the broader question of what

we were trying to accomplish [moreso] than would have been the case in a more narrowly focused effort.

Regardless of the size of the target market, the real importance of this approach was a focus on the business functionality rather than on the technical aspects of the system. As David Almeida put it:

> The real value that I saw in this was the focus on the business layer. Our chief systems architect, our chief systems engineer, and I focused on figuring out how to translate these requirements into business needs. We spent a tremendous amount of time and effort on that, in order to hand a "CONOPS" (concept of operations) over to our two systems engineers, who were really translating that CONOPS into the "shell" requirements at the systems level.
>
> Obviously, we had an understanding of how an order entry system works, but the question was how it works in a multi-domain telecommunications network that might span from the FAA to the DoD to civil agencies like the VA or NASA.
>
> And the more important question was how you extend the model to corporate requirements that are beyond those of traditional telecommunications to include enterprise-level services like voice mail or e-mail or cellphone-type services.
>
> So, that was the focus at the business layer, and that translates to systems engineers really taking those inputs and defining what the general system requirements were to achieve the business capabilities we had characterized.
>
> In order to accommodate our schedule we brought Inherit in a bit earlier than we might have otherwise, knowing that they would help us flesh out the rest of our requirements. So, we utilized their expertise in telecommunications, and in requirements management, as an added-value benefit.

PROJECT EXPERIENCE

The first stage of the project was gathering and capturing the initial use cases to determine the scope of what would be delivered. Based on the identified use cases, the project was divided into three iterations. During the first iteration, a subset of the PIM was developed, a PSM was generated from that PIM using the MDA Express tool, and then the application was generated from the PSM. The results were shown to the business user community to validate that the requirements had been met. In addition, the PSM was reviewed to give Harris an understanding of how the technical architecture would satisfy their technical requirements.

At times, the team would have to go back to the PIM, make some modifications to it, generate the PSM again, and then generate code. Those modifications became input to the next iteration, and all three iterations followed the same pattern.

Deployment started with the third iteration. In the deployment cycle, the code was handed over to the end-user organization for testing in their labs, and

Deployment, user testing, and system integration began with the third iteration

for integration with the application's back end. These labs are in a classified environment to which the Inherit people did not have access, so any issues that were experienced by the testers had to be reported back.

For some issues (e.g., for integration problems), the model transformation rules had to be tweaked. Harris would also provide feedback if there were any issues with a pattern that did not align well with their architecture or coding guidelines.

One other process within the project was working with the Harris technical staff to understand their design patterns and how they wanted the code to look—in terms of style and in the use of core J2EE design patterns as recommended by Sun. This required some changes to the transformation rules as well, followed by a demonstration that the changes met these technical requirements.

Several interesting things happened during the course of the MTSE project. Upon learning about the successful employment of MDA, Harris asked Rob Mitchell of Inherit to make a presentation about the MDA approach to directors and other senior managers at Harris. These people had heard good things about the MDA approach, and wanted to ask questions about the success of the current project, specifically in the area of integration.

One of the directors seemed to be very close to the project, and was aware that the code being generated was both well structured and conformant to the Harris coding guidelines. He said they had had virtually no problems in integrating our work with the back end. Rob Mitchell of Inherit gave us his reaction to this feedback.

MDA helps avoid the temptation of taking shortcuts that reduce code quality

We think this is one of the prime advantages of MDA. When a project finds itself up against a delivery deadline, the development team typically starts taking shortcuts. These shortcuts will get you to delivery but at the cost of producing lower-quality code that is much harder to integrate and maintain. And it is often the supplementary requirements that are tossed overboard in such a situation.

But with MDA, where the supplementary requirements are captured in the transformation rules, they are automatically included in the generated code, with little or no schedule penalty. The same patterns, etc, are embedded in all generated code, and the customer quickly learns the patterns and the structural philosophy they entail.

"Meta-debugging" is just one source of high-quality code

And this brings up another advantage of the MDA approach: the notion of "meta-level debugging." In this case, we had already removed most of the bugs in earlier versions of the Struts/EJB Archetype. As any new discrepancies are discovered you go back and fix the Archetype's transformation rules to address the problems. But because the generated code is so consistently structured, and reuses patterns repeatedly, when you fix such a problem that fix essentially ripples throughout all the generated code.

We went through several—probably six or seven—code generation phases before the final one, and in the end we delivered a significant number of lines of functional code, and they reported no problems with it. So, once you have your transformation rules correct you no longer generate bugs.

Another interesting aspect of MDA in this context is not about bugs per se but what might be called "mis-features." Most people who have been involved in software development have heard something like, "Yes, that is what we asked for but it is not what we want."

"Yes, that is what we asked for, but it is not what we want"

In this project, the ability to generate new executables quickly made it possible to get feedback from the business people while the requirements were still fresh in their minds. And there were indeed cases where the business people looked at a running prototype, checked the model from which it was generated, and then said, "Oh, yeah, that is what we asked for, and it is in the model, but it isn't really what we meant or what we want." As Rob Mitchell of Inherit put it:

In a sense, the quick generation of code that MDA enables is almost as good being able to run a simulation directly from the model. This is a huge benefit for many of our clients. And coupled with the ability to generate correct code because of the ratcheting effect of ever-better archetype-driven transformations we find that we can concentrate much more on figuring out whether the requirements were captured correctly. And this benefit increases proportionally with the size of the project, so the idea of using MDA to verify requirements has generated a lot of interest.

When I think about the impact that MDA has on this project, I think of three different levels. First, there is the ability to use MDA to win the business. We competed against companies that were not pitching MDA, and we were able to show productivity increases as well as stable architectures that can easily be integrated with existing systems. Some people claim that MDA is only appropriate for "green field" applications but this is not the case, as we demonstrated during the course of this project.

MDA benefits at three different levels

The second level is that from the customer's point of view there is a business concern: they need to get a product out the door. We can generate software very quickly using MDA, and we can improve the process of software development. Harris had a very skilled and effective software development team. The quality of their software was not an issue, because they had very effective processes and guidelines in place. But in this case, we offered them a business alternative that would allow the software to be developed more quickly.

The third level is that this approach is something we can show to our own potential customers, and provide assurance that we can show them how to quickly build—and then further customize—the software that they produce. So, this is how we build software and why we have an advantage over our competitors. We explained our view of this to Harris, and they decided they want to do the same thing.

We asked Rob Mitchell if there was much resistance to the adoption of MDA on the part of the Harris IT community. His response should be of interest to business people who might want to bring up the topic of MDA to their IT counterparts.

"Selling MDA to the Harris IT organization"

It was very interesting. Dave Almeida, the program manager, is a very forward-thinking person, and had the business benefits firmly in mind when the team chose the MDA approach. And he explained that very well to the software people, saying that MDA was an approach that the organization was going to try in order to see whether it worked. And as far as I could tell, everyone in the organization was on board.

We were brought in because Harris saw the business value of MDA, and in fact this parallels our experience with many customers. When we originally started our business and built our tool, we had an attitude of "if we build it, they will come."

We thought that architects, developers, and all technical people would just love it. But we found that wasn't the case at all. There were many objections from the technical people (for example, the "not invented here" syndrome or "your generated code can't possibly be as good as the code we write," etc.). We found that trying to sell MDA to technologists is an uphill battle.

But if you can show the business value of MDA to a business person in the organization, and they sponsor MDA, the technology people will grudgingly get on board. And once they get on board, the technologists often say, "This is great stuff!"

And you can see how their roles change. Instead of worrying about software "plumbing" issues they can now focus on more value-added issues. They become interested in things like "How do I write archetypes?" They find themselves at a level of development, or meta-development, that they were unaware of before, and they become very interested in it.

But what may happen instead is that the technology people see MDA and say that they don't need it, they can do all that on their own and can be just as productive. The business people are at the mercy of the technologists in cases like this, because the business people don't understand the technical issues well enough to say the technologists are wrong. Firing all the technology people is obviously a nonstarter, so this basically becomes a political issue in which the technologists look for reasons why it won't work and search for areas in which it may have failed to deliver.

The key at Harris was having a business-oriented champion, who saw the value of MDA in achieving his business vision for the company. This is a company whose products are heavily dependent on software, and MDA provided a way to improve their software process and thereby improve their ability to develop products quickly.

One more point: Note that the archetypes we've talked about only work with our MDA Express tool. So, if we leave and take our tool with us Harris would have the archetypes we've developed but would not have any way to leverage these archetypes. We had to solve that problem because they wanted the archetype so that they could reuse the approach in this and other projects. And we did solve it, by licensing MDA Express to Harris.

We asked Robert Lario of Inherit what he thought were the important realizations that Harris reached about MDA during thecourse of the project. He said:

> *"The key at Harris was having a business-oriented champion, who saw the value of MDA in achieving his business vision for the company."*

An important realization had to do with traceability, from the requirements specification, to the PIM, down to the PSM, and to the generated code. We're talking about the traceability of requirements through every phase of the development process, which becomes really important as requirements change.

If you have that traceability, you can quickly assess the impact of a change because you understand the scope of that requirement and therefore its effect throughout the project. Also, they made specific comments about the quality and consistency of the code. Even though this project had many and various different aspects, the application of the Struts EJB Archetype allowed for uniform consistency and quality, which would not be expected for projects built by several different developers, each applying their own style and guidelines.

The benefit of this was that as soon as you understand how the software is to be organized and structured in one part you know it will be organized and structured in the same way in all parts. This meant that someone working on one part of the project could quickly move to another part and be productive immediately.

Harris specifically said that this consistency helped them accomplish integration. As they were taking our software and integrating it into their existing environment they felt that this consistency made integration a lot easier. Of course, this also helped reinforce the consistent application of design patterns and software best practices by the team, and this consistency was also evident throughout the application.

Finally, the quick feedback loop in the process of turning requirements into production software was also an important realization. Anyone involved in requirements specification could quickly see how well the implementation fulfilled that specification.

In many cases with other approaches to requirements capture, it takes a long time to see the impact of what you have done. In this case, we were able to shorten that cycle to a degree that people came to understand how important it was to have high-quality requirements. This was a real learning experience for the requirements analysts, and its success encouraged business users to become much more involved in the software development process.

There was one aspect that was as much of a surprise to us as it was to them. When they found out how quickly they could change something in the model and get running code, they began asking for more and more changes. It got to point that in later iterations it was difficult to get them to freeze the specification because they saw how quickly changes could be incorporated. And in the last week alone we went through several generations of the system in accommodating changes and new requirements.

We also asked Robert Lario what he found surprising about Harris's MDA adoption process. He said:

The biggest surprise for us was how open and accepting the customer was of the process. Of course, we have had MDA engagements before this one and since this one, but this project was unique in two ways. First, they had a real need—a real business "pain point," if you will—in that they had a large amount of work to do in a very short amount of time.

Traceability of requirements, consistency of pattern usage, and the quick feedback enabled by code generation all support software best practices

Could this be too much of a good thing?

We cannot stress enough the importance of the project manager being willing to take the risk to look beyond the current environment and not allow IT to control the decision-making process. In the past we have had success in demonstrating the concepts of MDA to a business community, and seeing that business community want to adopt MDA, only to be stymied by IT people who pushed back very hard when asked to use this process.

By approaching the use of MDA as a business decision, Harris overcomes the "Monet factor"

This goes back to what we call the "Monet factor." A lot of technologists that we have talked to, particularly developers, think that MDA is like asking Monet to paint by numbers and they just won't adopt or use it. So, the surprise here was how readily they adopted it, and how quickly the IT folks got on board. It was a great project.

Finally, we asked Rob Mitchell whether there was an event or episode that made it clear that Harris had "gotten it" with respect to MDA. His response:

I can think of three different episodes. The first one was on that very first day that we spent with the client before we were awarded the contract. We've described that day, but one detail we did not mention was that we generated 30,000-plus lines of code to support a working application that we could launch and lead them through.

We ran it right there in that meeting, right from the model, without writing a single line of augmenting code by hand. Their jaws visibly dropped. Until then, they had been wearing their poker faces. To us, that was a significant event.

The second event occurred after we had built the initial models. The first time that we did essentially the same activities that we did in the demo, but for their own requirements, they were surprised at how quickly those real-world requirements could be turned into a running application, and also surprised at the quality of the generated code.

"... we could create code of the same quality that would result if we had all the time in the world"

When you're trying to do things quickly, you often find yourself taking shortcuts. But the archetypes that we built into our tool, and the MDA process itself, meant that we could create code of the same quality that would result if we had all the time in the world.

So, they were visibly excited by how quickly we were able to take their real-world requirements and generate a prototype application. Here again, it may be that we created extra work for ourselves because this initial success heightened their level of enthusiasm. And when they saw how quickly we could do these things, I think the project scope grew a little bit as a result. We were able to respond to that successfully, but it was more than we had originally signed on for.

The third event was when they took the software we had produced and integrated it with their back end. They had existing code that was built and structured as Java/EJB.

They knew that we had tuned our archetype so that it would integrate well with their existing application, but were still surprised when they saw how easily the integration task went. So, while there were many realizations of the benefits of MDA these three were the real eye-openers.

RESULTS AND BENEFITS

The most obvious and important benefit of MDA in this project was that it came in on time and under budget. There were no reports of code defects, and this code was integrated with the application relatively seamlessly. The integration task took one week of clock time but only three labor-days of effort, and that included the task of bringing the generated code to the lab and compiling it and the integration itself.

The success of this particular task heightened the visibility of MDA throughout the organization, as well as heightening the visibility of the project and the target product. The MDA approach Harris adopted has become part of the sales pitch to potential customers for that telecommunications management product, so the use of MDA itself has become a competitive advantage.

Harris's MDA approach becomes a competitive advantage and marketing advantage

Some of the benefits of this project were less tangible. The morale and motivation of the team was enhanced because they felt they were working with leading-edge technology. The project took what had been a traditional approach to software development and made it very exciting. And it was a learning experience throughout.

Although Harris had done some modeling before this project, those models could be characterized as "two-dimensional" and had been used primarily as a communication device. When Harris saw models actually being used to drive the software development process, it gave them a new appreciation of the modeling function.

The separation of their business concerns from their technical concerns allowed them to see that they could take the intellectual property of the business and potentially generate different types of solutions from it; for example, a Java solution or a .NET solution. Thus, they saw how they could use MDA to bring their solution to a wider market.

MDA also led Harris to think about how they could expand the scope of their project beyond the telecommunications arena. They are now thinking about how they might provide this type of managed service for many other service-provisioning applications. In this way, it widened their view of how they could apply the technology that already existed in their application in entirely different ways.

MDA leads Harris to think outside the box for more general service provisioning

And of course Harris now recognizes the fact that they can get more done with less. Projects that would not have been viable due to budgetary constraints have now become possible. And the business unit that created the MTSE application now sees expanded use of MDA as an alternative to outsourcing software development.

ONGOING AND PLANNED USE OF MDA

We typically asked our case study participants about the ongoing and planned use of MDA, including any MDA cross-pollinating that may have occurred into other projects or corporate divisions. In this case, the answer we got was much bigger than we bargained for, and it is unfortunate that we do not have the space to do full justice to the topic.

In our first interview with David Almeida of Harris, we asked about other MDA efforts at Harris and touched on a number of related topics, including CORBA's widespread use in the telecommunications arena and the OMG's considerable effort on MDA support for CORBA.

David suggested that we talk to Lew Pearson, Chief Architect, New Development, for Harris's NetBoss Business Unit, about their MDA-related work on the back end of telecommunications applications (for Harris's NetBoss Element Manager product).

We took this suggestion and asked Lew Pearson how he was using MDA in his work. His response was:

MDA is applied to the telecom application's back end

> We are creating a model-driven network management platform [NetBoss]. Every network element, every device, and every system that is monitored is modeled as well. We use the OMG's Distributed Management Task Force (DMTF) Common Information Model as a modeling paradigm for modeling the devices to be managed. Our primary focus right now is in element management, but we're looking into doing network management and more enterprise management as well.
>
> We view our system as a platform, with management agents to manage the particular devices. At the time this "smart" management agent is created, each device is modeled. We're using UML to model certain aspects of these devices–or network elements, or systems–whatever the agent happens to manage. There are not too many UML tools out there that do what we need to do, so we decided to use IBM's Rational Software Architect for our UML modeling.
>
> In our modeling, we have the library of classes that DMTF provides out of the box. Using our UML modeling tool, we put them together. Eventually, we adopted a UML model that covers different aspects of this managed system. In order to do that, we had to extend the UML profile (we are using UML 2.0) and this gives us enough flexibility and power to do the kind of modeling we want.

After ascertaining that this back-end product would be offered to communication partners (including other Harris business units), as well as external customers, we asked whether this product was taking the same approach to downstream tailorability as the MTSE project did, and if so how that was received by potential customers. Lew's response was:

> Absolutely. That is one of our main reasons for using MDA–being able to deliver easily customizable systems. You can do this several ways. Without modeling, you can do your implementation dynamically. Or, you can present an understandable model to the users, so they can modify them themselves or change them on the fly. But this has absolutely been one of our goals.

> When we talk to some of our government customers, they are very much interested in the Common Information Model. There is also interest in the shared information model. But they like the whole modeling approach, especially modeling of the business domain, as well as the ability to sort of "introspect" the model to find out what is in there. They also like the fact that it has standard interfaces from a programming point of view, so that you can use XML and web-based management interfaces. They're very happy to see this.

The MTSE project used MDA to focus on the business requirements for the front end of Harris's telecommunications applications.Here, we see that Harris's NetBoss business unit is using MDA and modeling to address the required functionality of the corresponding communication application back end. So, in essence this business unit within Harris is working to formally model the entire telecommunications management network (TMN) "pyramid" (as shown in Figure 5.4).

Modeling the entire telecommunications management network pyramid

When we suggested to Lew Pearson that his group and David Almeida's group seemed to be working on two ends of the same problem, his response was:

> Right. He is looking at it from the top-down—what the customer requirements are. And we are looking at it from the bottom-up, saying that you can model the top layer but that top layer really has to talk with these bottom layers.
>
> We are approaching this from the bottom mainly because this is our next-generation product. The capabilities of the current product are mainly at the bottom layer—device management, network management, et cetera.
>
> His customers come from the service side. His customers want communication service from point A to point B, they want a certain service level agreement in place (quality of service), and they want to hide the devices they have to go through.
>
> But that top level has to communicate with those devices for provisioning and setup, and for the monitoring needed to achieve those high-level goals. If you don't have that bottom layer in place you can't do the top level. But you also want to hide that bottom layer from the customer—except for the customers who have operators down on the floor, who need that lower-level information. You have higher service-level users who really don't care. So, you need a multitiered model in which those levels are integrated in order to support multiple perspectives.

For the authors of this book, this was an "Aha!" moment for us! We suggested that this combined effort could serve as the poster child for the entire MDA concept: providing various levels of abstraction and modeling different domains in support of separation of concerns to address the particular tasks to be accomplished by a variety of different customers.

An "Aha!" moment for the authors–discovering the MDA poster child

In a second interview with David Almeida, we presented him with the proposition that his business unit was really modeling the entire TMN stack. David was careful to say that he could not speak for Harris as a whole but from the standpoint of the business unit that contains both groups he agreed.

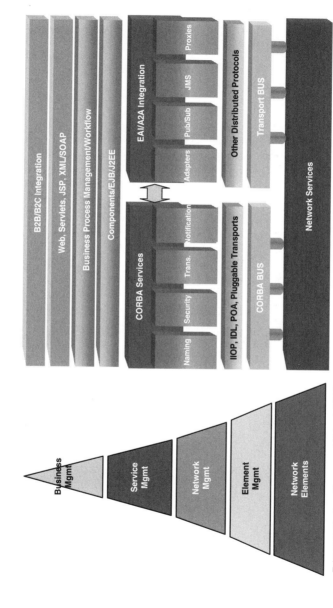

FIGURE 5.4 Telecommunications management network model.

Telecommunications Management Network (TMN) Model
Source: TeleManagement Forum TOM

I would most assuredly say that our direction in this particular business area [NetBoss] is very much in line with modeling the TMN stack–specifically in the development of what we call our "smart agents," which are the interface tools that actually talk to end devices on the network itself. From a technology direction perspective, I believe that we as a business area within Harris are very much moving in the direction of modeling the TMN stack such that we can get our customers to use modeling in order to manage their networks.

How does that fit into Harris Corporation's overall perspective? We are within Harris corporate architectures, so I think that to the degree that we are successful at penetrating the rest of the corporation–as being their network management tool for programs that they deploy to government customers, or on an element management capability for equipment delivered to end customers (our microwave division, or broadcast communication division)–the more successful we are at penetrating those businesses the more prolific the use of MDA will be at Harris.

TABLE 5.1 Project Profile: Managed Telecom Service Enterprise Project

Company/Organization	*Name:* Harris Corporation.
	Industry/function: An international communications and IT company, serving government and commercial markets to provide "assured communications" and information technology.
	Size: Annual sales of $3 billion, and employing more than 13,400 worldwide, including 5,500 engineers and scientists.
	Geographical reach/extent: Headquartered in Melbourne, Florida, Harris operates in more than 150 countries.
	URL: *www.harris.com*
QSP	*Name:* Inherit, LLC.
	Areas of experience/expertise: MDA Qualified Service Provider, concentrating on empowering organizations in the adoption of MDA. Expertise in project management, development methodology, and software architecture.
	URL: *www.inherit.com*
Business Pain Points	The need to change an existing telecommunications management application into one that could be tailored easily to meet the specific needs of various customers.
	Schedule pressure demanded maximization of IT staff productivity.
	The need for the new functionality to integrate smoothly with existing architecture and application.
Tools Used	Inherit MDA Express.
Model-based Artifacts Created	PIM.
	PSM.

6

CHAPTER SIX

DATA ACCESS TECHNOLOGIES/GSA: EXECUTABLE ENTERPRISE ARCHITECTURE

A large U.S. Federal Government organization creates an "executable architecture" that allows models to interoperate with existing systems. MDA's separation of concerns is a perfect fit for the federal approach to software development, and there is a plan to combine the disruptive nature of MDA with the disruptive nature of Open Source.

BACKGROUND

The U.S. Government's General Services Administration (GSA) "helps federal agencies better serve the public by offering, at best value, superior workplaces, expert solutions, acquisition services and management policies." GSA employs approximately 13,000 people and is the premiere federal acquisition and procurement agency, offering equipment, supplies, telecommunications, and information technology (IT) solutions to its customer agencies. GSA also plays a key role in developing policies used by other government agencies, and offers effective citizen-response tools and services.

GSA wants to create a single, executable enterprise architecture for dynamic simulation and interoperability

GSA's vision for meeting these responsibilities is OneGSA–a single executable GSA Enterprise Architecture to serve all of its customers. GSA chose MDA as the mechanism for creating this architecture, which consists of models that can dynamically simulate and facilitate interoperability between GSA Services and Staff Offices (SSOs) and external agencies. The goal is the dissolution of GSA "stovepipes" by essentially making the Federal Enterprise Architecture (FEA) operational within GSA.

This case study covers three related GSA projects: a proof-of-concept (POC), a pilot project, and the creation of the OneGSA Enterprise Architecture. The Daston Corporation, a prime contractor for GSA, ran the POC. Two MDA Qualified Service Providers, Data Access Technologies (DAT) and the LMI Research Institute (LMI), assisted GSA in the pilot project and the creation of the OneGSA architecture.

The goal of the POC was to demonstrate the ability to create FEA-compliant outputs with DAT's Component-X tool, which is an MDA-based tool that implements the OMG's Enterprise Distributed Object Computing (EDOC) and Component Collaboration Architecture (CCA) standards. The POC and OneGSA enterprise architecture projects in turn led to an MDA-based pilot project for the Federal Supply Service (FSS).

The FSS pilot was narrowly focused on modifications to an existing application in support of the acquisition function. These modifications were developed using the "MDA stack," and resulted in a simulation that could be run against and compared to a development version of the application. The preliminary OneGSA Enterprise Architecture was based on a high-level Computation-Independent Model (CIM) that cuts across all of GSA and describes the entire organization, primarily from a business perspective.

WHY GSA CHOSE AN MDA APPROACH AND WHAT THEY HOPED TO ACHIEVE

George Thomas is Chief Architect in GSA's OCIO Enterprise Architecture Group (OCIO stands for Office of the Chief Information Officer). Although his background is technical, he addressed the challenges he faced from a business perspective. George credits Chris Fornecker, his boss and GSA's Chief Technical Officer, for having the vision to support him in his efforts.

George's previous experience at various system integration shops included the use of UML to express system design (in the "UML as pictures" style, as he called it), but using UML models as documentation in this way resulted in the classic problem of having the system specification become out of synch with the code base.

About five years ago, when MDA was being developed, George and his SI colleagues became interested in how to do a better job of closing the specification/implementation loop. So, George came to the GSA—not with the responsibility to design, develop, or deploy code (as had been his past experience) but to take an architectural view in the pursuit of business goals. As he put it:

An architectural approach to closing the specification/implementation loop

Our objective was to take the ideas of MDA, with its capability to link all the various domain and physical and logical types of architectural asset abstractions, and use that to collapse the software development life cycle and make it more efficient.

GSA engages Data Access Technologies and LMI Research Institute

GSA outsources much of its IT work (like many U.S. federal agencies, GSA does not allow the vendor/contractor that gathers requirements or specifies a system to bid on that system's implementation). Ed Harrington, Executive Vice President of DAT, described how GSA came to engage DAT in support of this effort.

DAT was fortunate enough to meet George Thomas at an OMG technical conference. We had the opportunity to talk with him about what DAT in particular was doing with MDA. His interest, which was from a top-down business approach, became much more focused on EDOC and its approach to the development of enterprise architecture based on roles and collaboration.

    He saw that it would be a very good fit for at least an OCIO view of the organization. More importantly, this is a fit that has been successfully communicated to the business people. The role/collaboration view has been instrumental in validating the top-level OneGSA work done so far, and in continuing the validation of requirements in the follow-on work for their financial management line of business.

GSA also engaged the LMI Research Institute. LMI is a consultant to the government and has significant expertise in the functional domain of GSA operations. LMI did much of the data collection for the domain analysis, and helped GSA validate the formal models. In all three projects, DAT was responsible for creating the formal models and LMI acted as the prime contractor.

CHALLENGES

GSA had three concrete goals at the start. The first was a POC project in which MDA principles were applied to relatively simple tasks for the Office of the CIO, demonstrating Component-X and the power of the EDOC standards to develop enterprise architecture.

    The second was a pilot project in support of the FSS that was to modify an existing acquisition application. The third was the creation of the OneGSA enterprise architecture (described as "a mile wide and an inch deep") that aligns with the FEA.

MDA projects in an environment of mandated change

These goals were chosen and set in an environment of significant change at GSA. The mandate for these changes included the following initiatives.

- "Get-it-right" (initiative for better acquisition)
- Merger of two internal GSA organizations, Federal Technology Services and Federal Sales and Services, into a single Federal Acquisition Services organization

- Restructuring to provide a unified face to the customer
- Office of Management and Budget (OMB) and Congressional mandates and changes of mission
- Integrating and modernizing financial management
- Reduction of redundant processes and systems

It was clear from the outset that accommodating these initiatives would entail huge changes to the organization, to supporting systems, and to the skill sets of the GSA staff. And although GSA management realized that these changes would be risky, costly, and difficult, they also realized that it was simply not practical to attempt this change without addressing the costs and inefficiencies of their current redundant stovepipe systems.

MDA addresses "model to integrate" and "architectural rapid application development" environments

Therefore, GSA also wanted to use MDA to address a number of higher-level goals, including the creation of *model to integrate* and *architectural rapid application development* (ARAD) environments. To achieve these goals, GSA embraced the notion of an executable enterprise architecture that would combine MDA design-time and SOA (service-oriented architecture) runtime toolsets.

The executable enterprise architecture consists of models that dynamically simulate and facilitate interoperability between GSA SSOs and external agencies. In other words, models are executed to simulate the evolution and optimization of business process collaborations and are tested prior to procurement or development.

"Procurement *or* development" is the operative phrase here, because the GSA's goals embraced not only the "collapsing" of the software development life cycle (SDLC) but of the capital planning and investment control (CPIC) process as well. As George Thomas said:

Collapsing both the software development life cycle and the capital planning and investment control process

We try to communicate in ways that make sense to our EA constituents: CPIC and system or software development life cycles. These are things that people in our environment understand, so trying to collapse the time and resource burden associated with those life cycles for capital planning and software development have been key "better, faster, cheaper" messages for us.

This is all part of the story of collapsing the system development life cycle, and part of a larger initiative where the people in the federal government and GSA are talking about model-based acquisition. What we're trying to express is that the architecture process, using MDA techniques, is in fact the inception and the elaboration part of a typical SDLC.

When you're doing capital planning, and you want to make an investment, the first question we want asked is, "Do you have a CIM? Is there a business model that expresses the functional responsibilities of the system or the software that you are trying to get a budget for?" If not, you develop one in the inception phase. This business model talks about collaborative role interaction, and the opportunity is to see how that fits in across the enterprise as a whole.

By deriving technical requirements from business requirements, rather than vice versa, GSA is regaining control of its destiny

Finally, GSA faced a challenge common to federal agencies. GSA has few in-house technical resources, so many of their technical capabilities are outsourced. While GSA establishes the ground rules, policies, and environment in which the technology operates (and although they may own a lot of technology), for the most part this technology has been developed by commercial vendors. Recently, the goal has been to use commercial off-the-shelf (COTS) products as much as possible.

This has caused some difficulties, because it requires GSA to force-fit its business requirements into what is available from vendors. What they are trying to do now with MDA, value chain analysis (VCA), and SOA is to regain control of their own destiny. The OneGSA effort is an example of this in its goal of deriving the technology requirements from the business requirements and not the other way around.

EXPANDING GOALS

When we asked George Thomas whether the goals of a project changed as his organization became more familiar with MDA and what it could achieve, his first response was to say that it is not uncommon for the goals of a project to expand. We laughed, and we agreed, but when we pressed for the MDA-related aspects of this phenomenon he said:

Executable role interaction models improve communication with business experts about information flow within a business process

> We were initially interested in the capability for subject matter experts to be able to look at the executable artifacts, which is why we were very interested in the implementation DAT had done of EDOC standard [a forerunner of, and now part of, OMG's MDA] with their Component-X tool. The opportunity to execute and then step through, step into, and step over a collaborative role interaction model was something we found very useful for communicating with business subject matter experts about what information is flowing—in what context, and with what constraints—at any point in a process.

Traceability: business requirements to implementation technology—and performance metrics to business outcomes

> Because of the formalism of the modeling technology used—the implementation of EDOC in Component-X—that simulation allows us to refer to this as an executable artifact. So, we started to explore what an executable architecture could do for us. That allowed us to expand the goal of what we had been calling "executable EA" to "executable FEA." This is where we took the Federal Enterprise Architecture reference models and treated them as an aspect of the collaborative role interaction models we were using in the Component-X EDOC tool. So, that was one of our first goal expansions: from simulations to executable FEA.
>
> That was important because it gave us an opportunity to understand how to depict and demonstrate this notion of "line of sight" in the performance reference model, which is the umbrella reference model from the FEA. Line of sight refers to the ability to trace metrics from the business requirements all the way through to their implementation in technology.

This meant that an executable target model could interact with an existing system in our IT infrastructure. We could annotate those interactions with performance reference model metrics, which are time and cost reduction metrics that roll up into business outcomes.

We were able to show that if there was a system in our existing portfolio that was enacting a role in a target model that the metrics for cycle time—for example, in looking at this target business process scenario—could actually be captured, and reports generated from a baseline "planned/actual/achieved" perspective.

In other words, we could run an executable FEA simulation and then post-process that trace through the steps of the application, and see whether the metrics that we had annotated showed whether we were actually able to achieve such reductions. This was another goal extension, as we realized the capabilities of this notion of executable EA using the collaborative role interaction modeling formalism.

We were then able to expand this to talking about executable EA, executable FEA, and showing the explicit traceability of how a particular system is involved in performing the service, as part of the functional responsibility of a role that is interoperating/interacting with other roles in a collaboration. The traceability of the system that is associated with a collaboration, and is performing a service in support of a business outcome, was a powerful extension of the line-of-sight idea from OMB.

Ed Harrington of DAT also believes that the phenomenon of expanding goals significantly affected the course of the project.

All along, GSA had the vision and the desire to use MDA to separate concerns, to allow the business to drive the technology, and to allow the business to take advantage of technology changes when they happen. So, the whole concept of separation of concerns was a driving force. We are starting to get to the realization of this vision in the finance drill-down project.

Separation of concerns is a driving force

This project is about the retirement of a 30-year-old system running on a mainframe. That system supports all of GSA's receivables and billings, and fixed-asset accounting. In the finance drill-down project, we are developing the specifications needed to replace that system. The decision to undertake this project came about because of their increased understanding of MDA, and the ability of MDA-based approaches to communicate value.

In the development of the OneGSA project, we spent a lot of time with the finance group doing preliminary work at the business level. They began to see MDA's capabilities, and they ended up funding this finance project (jointly with the OCIO).

HOW MDA WAS USED

To recap, immediately after the POC project, GSA wanted to create the OneGSA Enterprise Architecture as well as a pilot project for the FSS in which an existing acquisition application was modified to conform to the OneGSA and FEA

MDA: The Source for OMB Compliant EA and eGov

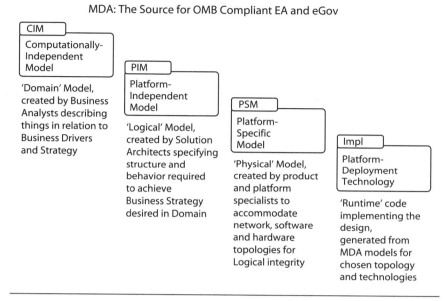

FIGURE 6.1   GSA mapping to MDA artifacts.

architectures. The OneGSA effort and the pilot project overlapped in duration, with the pilot beginning in the spring of 2004 and the first iteration of the OneGSA effort running from the summer of 2004 through the spring of 2005. So, how do these efforts map to MDA artifacts and processes?

As Figure 6.1 illustrates, the starting point for the GSA's MDA usage was the CIM. The standards MDA is based on, including EDOC, provide a framework for modeling the business. Those MDA standards also provide the means for transforming the models into actual working systems.

This means that you can focus on the business modeling with full confidence that having produced those models (and having gained all of the associated benefits from them) you also have the artifacts that allow you to move forward with building the system. Prior to this project, any GSA business modeling had been done separately, and (at best) then passed to IT for them to figure out what ought to be done with them. Ed Harrington characterized the new approach this way:

EDOC provides the framework for visual representation of business processes

It is an iterative and continuous process, and we are doing this with finance now. We take the CIM down through the PIM, and specify detailed system characteristics using both EDOC and other UML models. The data representation in finance is primarily in unconstrained UML, but the process representation is done in EDOC.

The CIM work was essentially a matter of creating a visual representation of business processes. In this CIM, *Community Processes* organize *Roles* in the context of shared objectives, and *Roles* are choreographed activities undertaken to achieve *Community Process* goals.

Roles initiate or respond to a collaboration *Protocol*, which describes a two-way conversation between *roles*. *Protocols* in turn choreograph *Ports*, and can contain nested subprotocols. Finally, *Data-typed Messages* flow over *Ports*.

Nouns are used to name Community Processes and Roles, and verbs (or "actionObject" phrases) are used to name Protocols. Names are chosen to describe action context and data content. These concepts are illustrated in Figure 6.2.

The use of a CIM was extremely valuable because it facilitated the involvement of the GSA business community. When we asked Ed Harrington specifically about the oft-touted MDA benefit of improving business/IT communication, he said:

> If by MDA you mean the EDOC approach we took to the business process, then MDA certainly facilitated this. Roles, collaborations, and activities made things pretty clear. By developing models focused on business roles and role collaborations, it was very easy for the users and business people to see, visually, where they fit within the models.

CIM encourages involvement of the business community and improves communication with the IT community

The Big Three: separation of concerns, traceability, and the ability to simulate at the business level

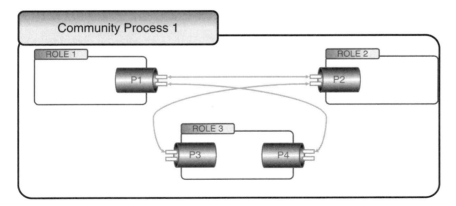

Color Legend:
- Community Process
- Role
- Protocol
- Port
- Data-typed Message

FIGURE 6.2 Process components.

By modeling the processes at the level of roles, collaborations, activities, and subactivities, you reach a level where you can very precisely describe what is going on in the business environment. People can see the roles they'll be playing as well as the relationship between systems and people. For example, at the CIM level we modeled the value chain processes irrespective of whether they are implemented in systems or by people.

While GSA could have done the "to be" modeling in other ways, the value here is that it could immediately be used to drive the next step of defining the system. MDA allowed us to reach the level of precision needed to take the models to the next step, down to the PIM, and enabled the development of specifications for the next level of system detail.

The point of all this is that with the MDA paradigm you must express the very detailed level of precision needed to take it to the next level of detail. For example, as we develop the PIM we may find that we have to go back and revise the CIM because we have not been precise enough.

And a very important point here is that the traceability inherent in the MDA approach is a big advantage. When you are working with the PIM, the trace between function and implementation is much clearer than was the case with traditional analysis methods. MDA gives you the ability—it almost forces you— to provide the FEA-mandated "line-of-sight" visibility between requirements and implementation.

The theme here is that we have the ability to remodel a very large enterprise, in a way that lets you achieve these downstream results with traceability. This is perhaps the most valuable and the most extraordinary result of these projects.

But there are other things as valuable; for example, the separation of design from implementation in support of federal regulations about awarding contracts to vendors for various aspects of a project. What MDA gives you that other approaches cannot is this: Anyone can say they will do an EA or separate the implementation concerns from design concerns. But MDA is unique in that it addresses all those requirements.

The three biggest MDA advantages are separation of concerns, traceability, and the ability to simulate—at the business level—and get agreement on the desired results before you write a line of code. And the third of these may be the most important, because not only can you get agreement on the correctness of the process, you also have the wherewithal to push this validated process down to the implementation level.

In theory, any simulation can be mapped to a real implementation. But if that mapping is not completely specified, or if it is not controlled by a standard, then you lose the traceability between the business-level agreement on the correctness of the process and the correctness of the implementation. In other words, you don't have a guarantee about the computability of the validated business process.

MDA provides the structure that allows the enforcement of things that facilitate the mapping to the downstream requirements. While these things could be done in other ways, it requires a great deal more focus and discipline because of the enforcement aspect that MDA can provide.

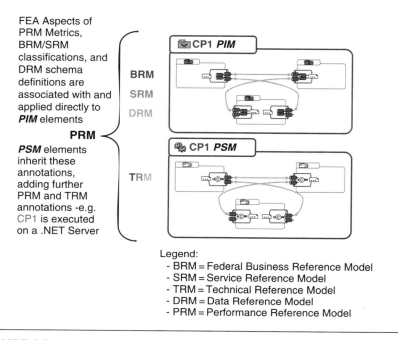

FEA Aspects of PRM Metrics, BRM/SRM classifications, and DRM schema definitions are associated with and applied directly to **PIM** elements

BRM
SRM
DRM

PRM

PSM elements inherit these annotations, adding further PRM and TRM annotations -e.g. CP1 is executed on a .NET Server

TRM

Legend:
- BRM = Federal Business Reference Model
- SRM = Service Reference Model
- TRM = Technical Reference Model
- DRM = Data Reference Model
- PRM = Performance Reference Model

FIGURE 6.3   Transformation from CIM to PIM to PSM.

Figure 6.3 illustrates the process of transforming the CIM to a PIM and then to a PSM. PIM-specific characteristics such as performance metrics and schema definitions are associated with CIM model elements, and then applied to PIM elements in the CIM-to-PIM transformation. Model elements in the PIM are assigned platform-specific characteristics, and these are carried forward in the PIM-to-PSM transformation.

PROCESS AND TOOLS

Because GSA outsources much of its software development, and because the companies that did the analysis/design for GSA cannot bid on the implementation work, there have as yet been no discussions about a specific software methodology for the eventual implementation of the system. But this is a bit misleading, because GSA has adopted a strong MDA-based approach to architecture, analysis, and design and because DAT's Component-X tool has been used heavily to generate code.

Component-X implements the OMG's EDOC/ECA-standard Component Collaboration Architecture. It is based on open standards, and supports a variety of technologies, including WSDL, ebXML, and JMS. Two other characteristics were even more important from the GSA's viewpoint: the tool's "tracing component" architecture (which supports explicit ties between design and implementation; i.e., line of sight) and its process simulation and dynamic modeling capabilities.

The Component-X tool is the enabling technology for GSA's Executable Enterprise Architecture

Component-X is thus the enabling technology for Executable EA, and has been instrumental in helping GSA achieve its goals. Component-X provided the ability to simulate processes within the GSA's actual IT environment–showing not just "box-and-line" diagrams but true simulation of process activities. George Thomas spoke highly of this tool's capabilities.

Models interact and interoperate directly with existing infrastructure

It was a good match for the architecture work we needed to do, and it was a good example of the kind of ideas we were trying to express about the central themes of MDA. We talk about "model-to-integrate," and we try to explain to people that these Component-X executable models are in fact Java programs. DAT has a framework and a library of code that takes these EDOC depictions and provisions them to Tomcat, a reference implementation of J2SE.

That capability–case tools on the Java standard, and the notion of model-to-integrate (which is a key idea behind MDA)–was another reason we really like the Component-X tool. Since these models were executed as Java programs, we could demonstrate interactions with existing service components.

The notion we're trying to put forth with this capability is that if we maintain the test domains of all the various IT initiatives across GSA then when the business architecture needs to show how a process interoperates with what exists a business model can go directly to, and interact with, the existing infrastructure. The executable model is a Java program and we can use the Java web services developer pack, and all the normal Java standards, for doing messaging. This was another powerful idea.

So, Component-X helped us to talk about Executable EA, which is a top-down, forward-engineering, push-it-from-the-model-to-the-runtime-platform approach (in the case of Component-X from an EDOC model to a J2SE platform). This let us show how we can collapse the CPIC cycle, with the relationship to the FEA as an aspect of the EDOC models.

And it also gave us the opportunity to interact with test domains to see how the existing infrastructure pieces play a part in target business processes. These were the reasons why we originally went with Component-X. Another reason was the expressivity of EDOC itself, and some of the other strengths of EDOC and the Component-X implementation in terms of composition.

So, if there are a set of roles, and business conversations or protocols that have been defined for those roles, the protocols and the roles themselves–seen as service components–are easily recomposed (or composed differently) for a new collaboration. This made it easy to talk about service component reuse using this tool and this style of modeling. This is why we started our business modeling effort using EDOC and Component-X.

DIVISION OF LABOR AND TRAINING

DAT participated in each of the three projects (POC, OneGSA, and FSS pilot). Daston Corporation was prime contractor on the POC, while DAT and LMI worked jointly on the OneGSA and FSS pilot efforts. LMI business analysts provided the value chain analysis, documentation of the as-is architecture (which was largely paper-based analysis; they did not model the as-is architecture in the same way they modeled the to-be architecture).

GSA personnel with direct involvement include three employees and five contractors from the OCIO. These people have provided project oversight from an earned-value analysis standpoint, and have implemented program reporting to ensure that the project remains on track.

The projects have relied on a mix of subject matter experts (SMEs), including both LMI and GSA personnel. Building the OneGSA Enterprise Architecture required interaction with many GSA SMEs to validate the OneGSA high-level architecture (there were multiple sessions with as many as 30 people involved).

Because of the GSA's reliance on contractors, much of the involvement by GSA personnel was part-time and intermittent—by SMEs who validated the modeling and analysis work of various contractors. George Thomas dedicated part of his time to the project, and one person from Finance dedicated 20% to 25% of her time.

Some of this interaction was led by the Project Management Office, which set up the meetings and provided facilitation support. At other times, DAT relied on LMI and their extensive business contacts within GSA to get things done. Ed Harrington gave credit to the MDA approach for the success of this work.

> As for the help MDA provided in this communication, once we got people into the room together the models themselves readily facilitated communication and discussion. We had a number of lengthy intense sessions about the validity of the models. So, the models provided the key tool to describe the desired to-be state of the business, and for enabling the business people to understand this state.

DAT provided training and mentoring to GSA in a continuing education process. They conducted workshops and presentations, but the real education occurred during the process of validating models with SMEs. This entailed an initial hour or so of introducing the modeling process and defining the meanings of the various graphical modeling elements and associated notation. DAT has trained several GSA people in the use of the Component-X tools so that they can create models and modify those that DAT created. Thus, rather than formal classes the training/mentoring effort so far has been a learn-by-doing exercise in on-the-job training, with GSA providing supervision over the process.

MDA AND THE FEDERAL GOVERNMENT'S SOFTWARE DEVELOPMENT APPROACH

The fit between MDA and the federal government's approach to software development is an interesting story, and one that illustrates the power and utility of "the separation of concerns" inherent in an MDA approach.

MDA as communication facilitator–this time between design/analysis and implementation teams

As mentioned previously, government rules preclude analysis/design vendors from bidding on the implementation work. MDA's separation of concerns fits this approach well because it allows a much more efficient handoff of information from the design/analysis team to the implementation team. As Ed Harrington put it:

> This is why MDA's separation of concerns is of such great value when working with the federal government. If you want to do such work, and you must separate the implementation details from the specification (and you usually do), this is a fine way to go about it.
>
> The reason for these rules is to prevent a large system integrator from creating a specification that only they can implement. So, in a very real sense MDA is an enabler for companies that want to participate in this business. And it illustrates the fact that separation of concerns is not simply something of abstract interest in the IT organization.
>
> Here, it is a necessity from the business viewpoint. So, MDA is a powerful enabler in a very large business segment–the federal government. And as GSA goes, so will go much of the national government, and many local governments and quasi-public organizations as well.

System specification in the form of MDA models provides a very efficient way of handing off analysis/design work to an implementation team, because when separation of concerns is maintained no platform-specific details are there to confound the creation of the executable system.

MDA tools capture and enforce GSA's software development guidelines

But the Component-X tool's ability to generate executable models (in the form of Java programs) presents an interesting wrinkle to this approach. Even though none of the code generated by Component-X is likely to appear in the as-built system, that code provides a great deal of value downstream.

First, the executable models have been validated by business SMEs as correctly implementing the requirements, and have been proven to interoperate with the existing infrastructure. So, they serve as "reference implementations" of system components for the implementation team.

Second, because the generated code is produced by a customizable "transformation engine" (which is true of almost all generative/transformative MDA tools, not just Component-X) the constraints embedded in the engine embody a great deal of knowledge about GSA's standards and guidelines for implementation code. Typically, this knowledge is lost when analysis/design artifacts are transferred to the implementation team, and it must all be relearned during implementation. But in this case, those coding constraints and guidelines are available to the implementation team, at least to the extent that they have been captured in the customized Component-X transformation template. George Thomas described the fit between MDA's support of traceability and GSA's goals for "model-based acquisition."

Model-based acquisition is a key GSA business goal

> In the circles of those who understand the value proposition of MDA, this is referred to as model-based acquisition: how we conceive of, procure, develop, deploy, and manage IT to support citizen-centric e-Gov. And it is one of our key business goals to do a better job here.
>
> We have experienced the classic gap, where the business people come in and say that there is something you need to do that doesn't map to your organization. Then architects come in and design a system and hand it over to coders. Basically, everyone ignores what the guy further up the chain has said. So, the explicit traceability that is part of the central MDA message, as you walk from one abstraction to another, or to some concrete artifact, is very attractive to us.

PROJECT EXPERIENCE

Again, this case study covers three different MDA projects undertaken by GSA. The first was the POC, the second was the FSS pilot, and the third was creation of the OneGSA Enterprise Architecture (the OneGSA Enterprise Architecture is described in the "How MDA Was Used" section). The OneGSA Enterprise Architecture project started in July of 2004 and ended–to the extent that any enterprise architecture effort can end–in March of 2005.

For the POC, Value Chain Analysis (VCA) was performed on the order-to-payment process and was undertaken in the fall of 2003. Again, the purpose of the POC was to ensure alignment of the OneGSA Enterprise Architecture and the FEA.

EDOC-based collaborative role interaction modeling was undertaken to accomplish this project, and this interaction model was annotated with aspects of FEA reference models. FEA reference models describe or represent the way in which federal agencies report their budget requests. So, in many ways the FEA is a taxonomy the OMB uses to understand budget requests for IT development, modernization, and enhancement.

This was the GSA's first business use case, and once it was possible to apply the FEA reference models directly to the target business interaction models the goal of "collapsing the capital planning and investment control cycle" became a reality, at least in this process. Instead of a manual word-processing-intensive process, OMB submissions could be expressed as an XML schema–taxonomy–applied directly to GSA models. As George Thomas put it:

GSA's first business use case: automatically reporting the relationship of a model to the FEA

> We had the capability to automatically report, from the models, the relationship to the FEA. And so we applied that in what is the principal role of enterprise architecture

in federal agencies, which is to help do capital planning and investment control. We have a requirement to talk to OMB in a certain way, and we needed to make that useful and correct as we move toward service orientation and all those wonderful things.

The submission process itself is not yet completely automated because the systems that capture and contain that information are not yet capable of automatically inserting submissions. But GSA has automated its end of the process, and in any case end-to-end automation of this process was not the primary goal. As George Thomas put it:

> The point is not so much that we can generate an automated report. It is that we are making a better link between the actual target knowledge base and the FEA directly, rather than having a manual process where people just get out the OMB-300 form and start typing.
>
> We wanted to be able to supply them with the relationship between what the architecture says about the requirements for this initiative and its relationship to the FEA taxonomy. That was one of the first things that we automated.

VCA proved to be an effective way of engaging business organizations, and of specifying business processes formally. Use of DAT's Component-X tool demonstrated the ability of MDA and EDOC to produce FEA-compliant output, and was instrumental in defining GSA's third MDA project, the FSS pilot project.

The goals of the pilot project were to achieve a cohesive approach to business planning via targeted enterprise architecture analysis/development and integrated business/IT planning. It provided for seamless collaboration and integration with the FSS's business partners, and it demonstrated the usefulness of dynamic models in a shortened design and development life cycle.

Specifically, the pilot enhanced the GSA's "eBuy" capability to include purchase order and task order management. By addressing a real-world problem—implementing the FSS order-to-payment capability in a way that accommodated both current and future states of the system—the project allowed eBuy to transition smoothly to support the target enterprise architecture and to be integrated with other functions in an SOA.

ORGANIZATIONAL DEVELOPMENT

We asked all of our case study participants whether, and how, the adoption and use of MDA had affected their organization. The answers we got in this case study were indicative of the vast difference between GSA (and government organizations in general) and the typical business enterprise. Nevertheless, George Thomas gave us some very interesting responses to questions in this vein.

For example, we noted in the "Challenges" section that the goals for GSA's MDA projects were chosen and set in an environment of significant change at GSA. We asked about the organizational transition implied by those goals and requirements, and how it would affect the communities attached to previous approaches: How is that transition going? How does it impact those cultures? How do people react? How do you deal with the inevitable pushback? George Thomas replied:

Those are really tough questions. Clearly it is disruptive, and some of the capabilities espoused by our use of MDA and by MDA in general may force some well-established support companies to think about their business model a bit more.

MDA can be disruptive, especially in a decentralized organization

We've heard things like, "As if global outsourcing wasn't bad enough, you guys are now trying to commoditize the creation of code!" So, it certainly is disruptive, and I don't think that we as an organization have any magic pixie dust that makes this any easier.

It sometimes happens that you get mixed up in the technical issues of doing model-driven architecture at some of the most mundane levels. For example, "Well, UML2 can do this, but none of the UML tools currently implement that capability, or if they do the way that they serialize it for import and export requires some sort of intervention to deal with idiosyncrasies."

Unless you adopt a particular pragmatic set of conventions about the precise syntax and semantics of what architectural view is used and where, and develop your tool chain around that, then there are many, many different ways to skin the cat, with many tools, meta-models, and approaches. And that amount of choice begins to be a difficult technical problem.

I think that the OMG is aware that the set of meta-model standards they present is both a blessing and curse. It is a blessing in that there are standards that are well conceived by very smart people, and it is a curse in that they are often overlapping and redundant. And in some cases, their semantics are not clear.

"The set of OMG's meta-model standards is both a blessing and a curse"

So, a turf war may happen, say over a particular methodology that is lucrative to a given support vendor. When such a vendor becomes aware of someone else's approach to, say, model-to-integrate, it's easy for them to confuse things with technical idiosyncrasies and the very nature of all this meta-model stuff.

That is not the kind of happy talk you usually see in a case study but it is reality. If I, or anyone within any single agency, were in a position to say, "This is how we're going to do everything (from inception, to elaboration, to construction, to transition within IT) in order to align it with the business and achieve better agility," then we would have none of these issues.

But instead, all of our environments, and all of our constituents, are … well, we say "federated" on a good day and "decentralized" on a normal day. So, the amount of work in dealing with conventions of syntax and semantics—in order to maintain the desired amount of tool and platform agnosticism that MDA espouses—is very resource intensive. That is a kind of counterbalance and reflects that we are in the early stages of MDA adoption.

We suggested that whenever a new technology is adopted it is disruptive, and that its ability to be fully successful is in large part based on its maturity. George Thomas agreed.

Yes, and in our case that maturity, as well as the understanding of that maturity, is spread across an extremely decentralized organization. Every GSA line of business has its own CIO. Every CIO has an organization that does things, with greater or lesser success, or maturity, or advanced techniques.

There isn't anyone who can just say "This is how we're going to do it" and just streamline all of that. We can do that individually, but across the organization at large you can't.

"So, having drunk a lot of the Kool-Aid, I can't really think of anything to which the principles of MDA could not be applied."

We then asked whether there were any likely "sweet spots" for MDA adoption. He replied:

What we've been saying about MDA is basically the same as what I heard Gartner say at a recent SOA/BPM conference: MDA represents a kind of umbrella management context for everything from the entire software life cycle to the implementation of a system of initiatives in support of a business initiative. So, having drunk a lot of the Kool-Aid, I can't really think of anything to which the principles of MDA could not be applied.

But we took the opportunity to ask this question in a different way, because even though GSA does not have formal authority over other government agencies, it is doing its best to encourage the use of MDA. We were given a copy of GSA's "One GSA Enterprise Architecture Blanket Purchase Agreement and Statement of Work" (Solicitation No. GSA/TFL06-2064, Amendment No. 1 Correction) and an associated Q&A document as background material. The latter document contains a very interesting question and answer.

QUESTION 16: Are all GSA systems development initiatives using the Architecture Driven Modernization / Model Driven Architecture?
RESPONSE: All GSA system development initiatives are not currently using the MDA/ADM methodology. However, it is anticipated that all future Enterprise Architecture Program Management Office and Blanket Purchase Agreement task initiatives will use the methodology and tools.

But there is an MDA "sweet spot" at GSA: Business Process Management

After getting permission to cite this, and noting that the statement of work itself described VCA of business processes as "the primary discovery mechanism for developing the OneGSA Enterprise Architecture," we asked George Thomas whether all of this implied that business process management was such a "sweet spot" for MDA adoption in GSA and associated organizations. He replied:

First of all, with respect to that statement that is indicative of the decentralization we were just talking about. In other words, anything that comes from my shop goes down in this way. But that is not to say that everything that goes down goes through my shop.

That's the reality. What we are able to do as we show more value—for example, in the provision of a service component for the financial management LOB that is not available via COTS/GOTS—if they want to procure that capability and we say, "We already have the ability to generate the code and deploy it in a J2EE environment, so what is there to procure?", well, that will be disruptive moment.

But in terms of the sweet spot question, I think that business process management and MDA illustrates the point of recent Gartner statements about all these management ideas coalescing into Model-Driven Architecture. From our perspective—and what we focused on initially, and what is typically the most broken and least understood area, and certainly is very much in vogue—is a discussion of business processes.

So, our application of EDOC and its Component Collaboration Architecture focused on exactly that: what is the choreography, and what are the collaborative role interactions, in a business process that is one of many in the entire value chain. So, that was a functional sweet spot immediately, with this particular style of modeling.

That is more a reflection of EDOC and CCA and DAT's implementation of that than of MDA per se. For example, although there are a lot of executable UML tools and other wonderful tools, you don't typically see people simulating activity diagrams.

But to be able to describe the business process and the functional requirements of activities within that process, and then to see that activity as a service component and then provision that to a web-service/J2EE implementation, is definitely a sweet spot in terms of how you realize target business processes.

We suggested that the sweet spot exists because people are already interested in modeling business processes, and people are also interested in providing an SOA of some kind. What they don't typically have are a way of tying the two together clearly to specify how a process model maps to a set of services, and a way of simulating processes as a set of services. George Thomas replied:

Mapping process models to SOA, and then simulating processes as sets of services: MDA as a language for depicting business processes and their relationship to services

Right. When you can do that you have a better requirements specification, and a better alignment of what you are trying to procure with your actual capability. And the simulation part is what we refer to as the executable model.

The opportunity to realize that service better, faster, cheaper (thus collapsing the SDLC) is disruptive. And it's sort of where MDA came from. If you design a good model, you can generate a lot of the code. But we've used MDA as a sort of language for depicting business processes and the relationship to service orientation.

We also asked a follow-up question about the reaction of software development vendors to the GSA's intended use of MDA. The reply was:

MDA's role is not to generate code but to help get better results

The biggest result of that was to make our independent support vendors stand up and take notice: for us to say, "We think that this SOA depiction, which is explicitly linked to this model, and which we can generate and deploy as a service on this open-source J2EE container, can be done better, faster, cheaper than the two years and $800,000 you guys would spend writing some JSP."

That was probably the biggest impact. And again, this was not necessarily seen as a positive thing because the message that was received there was "this code generation thing is going to put me out of a job."

And of course it isn't our role as the Architecture group to generate code per se, but it is our role to show how advanced technology and techniques (such as those in MDA) help us get better results, either faster or cheaper and maybe even both. Another aspect of that was having the technology leaders (CIOs in other GSA organizations) themselves start to understand what it was, and start to commission their own studies of what was happening with MDA and how it might help their organizations.

For example, the work [. . .] done in the Finance LOB has been done mostly with us. And we have other business lines within the GSA that have commissioned their own MDA pilots because they are interested in different toolsets and meta-models. The value proposition that we were able to show encouraged them to do that.

And that's a good thing; it just takes a while. As I said, in a different organization (like a company), where the CEO says, "I believe what the CTO is saying and this is how we're going to do things," then the path to using MDA might be a lot shorter and results might be generated faster and more cheaply.

I don't have total control, and in some cases no control whatsoever, over how people actually do things and what they do with their money. GSA business lines act as fee-for-service organizations, and in fact they're paying my bills. So, it's a case of the golden rule, where he who has the gold makes the rules.

Demonstrating MDA's value proposition has led to further investigation elsewhere within GSA

What I have been able to do is demonstrate the value proposition of these ideas and that has led to further investigation on their parts. And it has led to the requirement for their support folk to say, "We understand, and this is what we can do for you along those lines, etc."

We then asked about the vendors who complained that code generation would put them out of business. The reply was:

It's gone from that initial reaction to: "Absolutely; we are expert MDA practitioners." That's probably the most positive effect, but at the sales pitch level we've at least gotten that into the lexicon. When it comes to the "simple matter of implementation details," the creativity inherent in the freedom of our approaches manifests itself, and that is not a bad thing.

We're not trying to be prescriptive, or to say there is just one way to do this right. There are many ways to do this right, and there are different things for different people to focus on.

We are focused on understanding an enterprise-wide business process, in a service-oriented depiction, and the use of that for capital planning. We'd like to make an explicit link to the people who realize, develop, run, and manage those services in the IT infrastructure, and there are many different ways to attack that problem.

We find that most often people want to start talking at the Platform-Specific Model level, and they want to start modeling at that level. They want to work on generating code for their favorite target platform.

But we are really starting at the highest level. We're trying to find the business abstraction that helps our executives understand the universe of buyer-agent-seller interactions.

But we want that to be done with a formalism that can be traced all the way down to running code. And we would love to think that configuration management becomes less about a code base and more about a model base, where we have a generation and provisioning capability from the model.

So, it generally has been a positive affect on the vendors. I think all the people now talking to the GSA at this point about what they do at least acknowledge an awareness of the MDA value proposition. But just because you do UML modeling doesn't mean you're doing MDA.

GSA started at the highest level of modeling, to provide a formal understanding of buyer-agent-seller interactions

We asked George Thomas, "Do you have any plans to assist other organizations in their understanding of or uptake of MDA?" He responded:

That is the focus and objective of the Open Source E-Gov Reference Architecture (OsEra) project. The OsEra project is an open-source environment for design and runtime tools, to realize the service specifications that have been modeled in the FEA and the financial management line of business efforts.

OsEra is not particularly relevant to this case study perhaps, but it is about the capabilities we've been discussing: the business model defines the collaborative role interactions, the logical model "componentizes" that across an n-tier environment, and the ability to generate executable specifications of that from the models—this is basically the core MDA story.

So, with OsEra we are trying to combine the disruptive business model of Open Source with the disruptive capabilities of MDA, and the end result harkens back to what I was saying about the FEA modeling work.

If we are able to design and elaborate a service that fulfills a business activity and process, and if we are able to provision that and deploy it to a mature enterprise-level standards-based middleware platform, we absolutely want to make the "best value" point, which is that we must understand what it is that we need to procure. That has been our focus—to get to the point where we can prove that we are not crazy to say that. And once we can do that, we simply want them to take these capabilities into consideration before they say, "We need ERP" or "We need CRM" or "We need SCO" or whatever large monolithic architecture COTS tool they would have gone off to buy.

So, we're really trying to get that into the thought process—what it means to be agile, what it means to get best value—with the capabilities of this MDA stuff, and with the availability of this open-source stuff. So, those are the ideas we are combining with the OsEra project, and we are using the work that we are doing

The Open Source E-Gov Reference Architecture combines the disruptive business model of Open Source with the disruptive capabilities of MDA

in enterprise architecture projects (such as finance management LOB services) to demonstrate that point.

So, we can say, "Here's the financial management line of business specification and you can use that in an RFP to procure things. And by the way, that specification identifies sixty work roles, which may have a number of components that are helper roles to fulfill that in a three-tier environment." And we can generate the BPEL choreography for each of these business processes and show you that they are in fact interacting with each other.

At some point, someone will ask what this is running on. And we will say, "Web services and J2EE." And they will say, "Okay, let me go buy something that gives me a web service and J2EE implementation of this model." And we say, "We already have that."

So, we are not able to say, "This is the way we'll do things," but we can say, "Doesn't this make a big difference in whether or not you want that $100 million solicitation?" And that's an important idea.

RESULTS AND BENEFITS

Although it is difficult to quantify the benefits GSA has obtained through the use of MDA thus far, it is very clear that as a result of MDA enormous change is on the horizon, even if it is just beginning to ripple through the organization. As for the specific results of the projects undertaken thus far, the creation of the OneGSA Enterprise Architecture was extremely significant. The OneGSA EA has become a business enabler because MDA and VCA can together map value-focused business processes with IT execution mechanisms and strategies. It is a simple case of better system definition leading to better systems. Because users can change or expand the definitions of processes, roles, and connections, there are fewer false starts, better communication, and increased interoperability and reusability.

The OneGSA Enterprise Architecture earns GSA a "green" rating from the Office of Management and Budget

In addition, OneGSA was an administrative and political win for the organization. "According to the White House website,[1] "The President's Management Agenda, announced in the summer of 2001, is an aggressive strategy for improving the management of the Federal government. It focuses on five areas of management weakness across the government where improvements and the most progress can be made."

This executive initiative calls for a results-oriented expansion of E-Government, and the Office of Management and Budget rates federal organizations annually on their implementation of the FEA. It assigns red to agencies that are failing, yellow to those that are making progress, and green to agencies that are where they should be at this point in time. GSA earned the green rating on September 30, 2005.

---

1   http://www.whitehouse.gov/omb/budintegration/pma_index.html

The purpose of the POC project was to ensure and demonstrate the alignment of the OneGSA EA with the FEA. EDOC-based collaborative role interaction modeling was undertaken to accomplish this. This interaction model was annotated, in the form of an XML schema, with aspects of FEA reference models. So, the proof in this POC was the demonstrated capability to report–automatically from the models–the relationship of the interaction model to the FEA.

In other words, the requirement was to be able to communicate with the OMB in a certain way. Not only was that specific requirement fulfilled, it was done in a way that provided line-of-sight visibility from requirements to implementation that demonstrated the ability to work with existing infrastructure and that supported reuse in an SOA.

Finally, the FSS pilot project created a set of roles and collaborations that modeled the execution of purchasing services, assigned business rules for these functions, and diagrammed choreographies that model information exchanges. The resulting system modifications allow FSS business analysts and IT personnel to interactively view data flows as well as processes, business rules, and interactions among roles. Thus, enterprise architecture and IT components have become a communication vehicle between the business and IT communities, and have clarified communication among the Office of Management and Budget, the General Accounting Office, and GSA. In the GSA, models have become the development and documentation tool of choice throughout the software development life cycle because they support GSA's moves toward SOA and allow rapid response to changing business environments.

Models are GSA's tool of choice for the software development life cycle because they allow business stakeholders to interactively view processes, roles, and interactions

ONGOING AND PLANNED USE OF MDA

When we originally researched this case study, we were told that GSA, DAT, and LMI were undertaking an additional MDA project in the finance area to address replacement of receivables/billing and asset management functions on a legacy mainframe system. Because this project had not been completed at the time, DAT and GSA were unable to provide details. They said only that this project was employing MDA tools and standards to extend the OneGSA Enterprise Architecture and was applying Architecture Driven Modernization tools for legacy analysis.

We have now been informed that this project was completed successfully in December of 2005. Unfortunately, our schedule did not allow us to interview the principals involved or to write a complete description of the project.

However, DAT and GSA provided some information about this Financial Management Enterprise Architecture (FMEA) project, which was sponsored by Offices of the Chief Information Officer and Chief Financial Officer at

GSA and carried out under the umbrella of the OneGSA Enterprise Architecture program. In this project, GSA has developed the specifications needed to replace the legacy mainframe system mentioned. Project deliverables included the following.

- A target business architecture for consistent and comprehensive financial management, supporting all GSA services and staff offices
- A logical system architecture for a cohesive financial management suite supporting the business architecture, particularly where functions had to be transferred from existing legacy systems
- A set of interface definitions to act as the basis for a standard GSA financial management SOA

The benefits delivered by this project include the following.

- A set of system and technology specifications that match their associated business requirements
- Traceability up and down the MDA "stack"
- Specifications for services acquisition (buy or build)
- The adoption of models as the primary architectural artifacts
- A modernized–, non-stovepiped–, service-oriented basis for moving forward
- The ability to implement these specifications over time (thus avoiding any "Big Bang" events)
- Assurance that these FMEA functions can be integrated with other GSA and non-GSA services
- Prevention of lock-in to proprietary vendor architectures
- Providing a self-documented system
- A framework that allows for strategic evolution of business processes and information systems, rather than the usual piecemeal growth of patchwork solutions

As might be guessed, there is another ongoing MDA project at GSA: that of writing a more detailed version of the OneGSA Enterprise Architecture. DAT is the prime contractor for this project and is currently working with a number of subcontractors.

TABLE 6.1 Project Profile: Executable Enterprise Architecture

---

Company/Organization *Name:* U.S. General Services Administration.

Industry/function: GSA is the premiere federal acquisition and procurement agency, and helps federal agencies better serve the public by offering expert solutions, acquisition services, and management policies.

Size: GSA employs approximately 13,000 people.

Geographical reach/extent: USA.

URL: www.gsa.gov

QSP/Consultants *Name:* Data Access Technologies, Inc.

Areas of experience/expertise: A MDA Qualified Service Provider, DAT architects and implements products and technologies that enable global Internet computing for the enterprise. DAT is a leader in the efforts to make the standards required for enterprise components open and interoperable. Much of the technology offered by DAT is a direct result of a grant from the Advanced Technology Program of the U.S. National Institute of Standards and Technology.

DAT helped create the OneGSA Enterprise Architecture and provided the Component-X tool for the creation of executable models that dynamically simulate and facilitate interoperability with existing systems.

URL: http://www.enterprisecomponent.com/

Name: LMI Research Institute.

Areas of experience/expertise: An MDA Qualified Service Provider, LMI is a not-for-profit strategic consultancy committed to helping government leaders and managers reach decisions that make a difference. LMI assisted GSA in the pilot project and the creation of the OneGSA architecture.

URL: http://www.lmi.org/

Name: The Daston Corporation.

Areas of experience/expertise: The Daston Corporation provides customized information technology, financial management, and management consulting solutions. Daston is a prime contractor for GSA, and ran the first proof-of-concept project.

Business Pain Points OneGSA architecture was undertaken in an environment of significant change, including the merging of two internal organizations, and various mandates from the U.S. Congress and the Federal Office of Management and Budget.

(Continued)

TABLE 6.1   Project Profile: Executable Enterprise Architecture—Cont'd

	The need to restructure systems to provide a unified face to the customer.
	The need for the new functionality to integrate smoothly with existing architecture and application.
	The need to integrate and modernize financial management.
	The need to reduce redundant processes and systems.
Tools Used	DAT's Component-X.
Model-based Artifacts Created	CIM.
	PIM.
	PSM (in the form of executable models).

7

CHAPTER SEVEN

INTERACTIVE OBJECTS/DAIMLER CASE STUDY: AUTOMOTIVE INDUSTRY

A major player in the auto industry uses MDA to build a support system for all processes within production plants, replacing 10 legacy systems and leveraging existing architecture and infrastructure. "Model-driven offshoring" produces organizational integration with remote development partners.

BACKGROUND

DaimlerChrysler is a powerhouse in the automotive industry, with products that range from small cars to sports cars to luxury sedans, and from vans to heavy trucks to coaches. With more than 38,000 employees worldwide, DaimlerChrysler sold more than 4 million passenger cars and more than 700,000 commercial vehicles in 2004, with revenues of €142.1 billion ($192.3 billion).

This project was undertaken with DaimlerChrysler TSS GmbH (TSS), which is a wholly owned subsidiary of DaimlerChrysler AG, founded in 1998. TSS specializes in J2EE- and .NET-based applications, Lotus Notes, and data warehousing solutions, as well as consulting and test services—all done exclusively for DaimlerChrysler AG worldwide.

Interactive Objects Software GmbH, founded in 1990, is an IT solutions company that has made the application of Model Driven Architecture (MDA) its specialty. Its customers include many Fortune 500 companies in various industries, including finance and insurance, transportation, government, software, telecommunications, and automotive. Interactive Objects is an MDA Qualified Service Provider and has been an OMG member since 1990. The company has won numerous awards for its ArcStyler architectural platform and for the applications that have been built upon it.

The project undertaken by TSS and Interactive Objects was called Electronic Production Planning (ePEP) and its purpose was to provide support for all processes within production plants, from construction clearance to production clearance. The ePEP modules include the following.

The Electronic Production Planning (ePEP) project provides support for all production processes in all plants

- Global Parts/Schedule Alignment (GTTA) to ensure timely availability across different production sites of new or changed parts
- Construction Plan Change Management (KOAEND), which uses a customizable rules engine to distribute incoming construction plan change information to all stakeholders
- Production Coordination (ESKOORD), which supports the entire production process chain, including work order management, master data management, automatic distribution of supplier queries, quotation management, purchase order management, and delivery schedule management

WHY DAIMLER CHOSE AN MDA APPROACH AND WHAT THEY HOPED TO ACHIEVE

Daimler TSS began investigating MDA approximately 14 months before the start of the ePEP project, by creating a small team to investigate the various MDA options available in the market. They were unsure whether they needed an MDA or Model Driven Development (MDD) approach, but they had the clear goal of using models.

They were looking for several advantages. First was the ability to leverage their existing architecture and IT expertise. Second, they wanted to bridge the communication gap between their business and IT communities. And third, after a suggestion by the Interactive Objects team they began to see the potential of applying a model-driven approach to their practice of "offshoring" some software development work to their software development partner's site in Kuala Lumpur, Malaysia. The process of choosing a consulting partner involved an examination of tools (TSS tried several), as well as an evaluation of a potential partner's overall technical strategy and its ability to provide supporting professional services.

TSS had no interest in a tool or IT infrastructure that would replace or disturb their existing sophisticated J2EE-based Application Framework and Infrastructure (known as PAI) or their current software development processes, which are CMMI certified. They needed a tool that would fit their current architecture and process such that both would be able to accommodate future changes and architectural requirements.

ePEP addressed the "how" of implementation as well as "what" was actually to be implemented

In other words, it was not simply a matter of what would be implemented in ePEP but of *how* it would be implemented and how it would fit into the existing IT landscape. And finally, TSS did not want to become dependent on any external organization.

TSS came to the conclusion that Interactive Objects offered the best value. One reason was the capability and flexibility of Interactive Objects' ArcStyler tools. Other factors were Interactive Objects' extensive experience with large enterprises, as well as their ability to support TSS and react very quickly to their needs (which they demonstrated immediately by supporting a small pilot project).

Interactive Objects also helped TSS achieve their objective of maintaining self-sufficiency. For example, as a result of the Interactive Objects partnership TSS now has a staff of experts capable of introducing the MDA approach elsewhere in the organization. That process is under way and going very well.

The challenges that faced the ePEP project were clear. The application itself had to implement very complex business and process logic, and it had to be distributed both geographically and organizationally. It had to replace the functions of more than 10 different legacy systems while being integrated within a complex IT landscape. And TSS set a goal of a 10% improvement in development productivity for the MDA process itself.

EXPANDING GOALS

TSS's goals expanded throughout this project, and they are still evolving. Essentially, they want to "tighten the screw one more turn" in order to be able to generate more code, to automate as much as possible, and to introduce improvements to the modeling style so that they can reduce the risk of potential misunderstandings—both between the IT and business communities and between the local and offshore software development organizations.

We asked Wolfgang Käfer, Senior Manager and Chief Technology Officer of DaimlerChrysler TSS, whether the goals for MDA expanded as the organization became more familiar with it. His response was:

> Yes. When we started with MDA we had in mind improving efficiency and consistency, and improving our abilities in offshore development with particular emphasis on IT infrastructure as defined by J2EE. We are now looking to expand MDA's use both in terms of the presentation layer and in the ability to generate more code.
>
> Beyond that, we know that we want to get more out of MDA, and we are convinced that we can do that, but we are not yet sure exactly how we will go about it. But we are confident that we can expand the use of MDA to include other architectural layers, and that we can get more benefit from MDA in the layers we are working with today.

TSS also believes that it can reduce costs by enforcing corporate governance over software architecture. The goal here is to achieve architectural consistency and stability across the entire organization, and the success of the ePEP project is helping TSS realize that goal.

In addition, TSS wanted to improve the processes that control what happens when an application is turned over from the IT department to another organization. TSS does not believe that an organization should take responsibility for an application unless it is well documented and maintainable. Here again, the application of MDA has resulted in changes beyond the originally intended scope, and in benefits to the entire organization rather than just to architects, designers, and developers. Alberto Perandones, Director of Professional Services at Interactive Objects, characterized the MDA-related maintenance advantages as a particularly important driver of the expansion of goals.

Corporate governance over software architecture benefits many stakeholders

> While you can suggest to the customer that MDA benefits productivity in software development, some studies suggest that 80% of the IT budget typically goes toward maintenance of existing systems. Note that maintenance is part of the "strategic" budget because it governs the operation of systems in support of business, whereas the development budget is not strategic. If you can demonstrate that MDA can influence this strategic maintenance budget, then you have access to the people who control that budget—and this can result in many new project opportunities.

HOW MDA WAS USED

The ePEP project used MDA in three main ways. First, they used Interactive Objects' ArcStyler software to create customized "cartridges" that together provide a custom MDA architecture blueprint for their existing PAI framework, as shown in Figure 7.1.

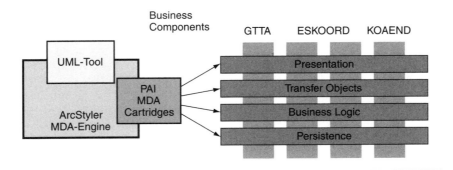

FIGURE 7.1 MDA architecture blueprints.

Second, TSS created a platform-independent system model, which was enhanced with MDA "marks" to capture the technology characteristics and requirements of the DaimlerChrysler PAI target platform. These models were invaluable for coordination between TSS's local and remote development teams, as discussed in material following. But TSS continues to maintain these models and keep them synchronized with the code because they are valued strategic assets.

UML is used largely by the technical team

We asked Wolfgang Käfer how requirements were captured. His answer touched on the use of UML among various communities, as well as the specifics of requirements gathering.

In this project, we follow the general DaimlerChrysler guidelines (known as HBSG) as well as TSS-specific guidelines on how to develop systems. UML plays a role in these guidelines but not a central role. Along with UML, a requirements list (for example, maintained in Requisite Pro) is used by the technical team in order to have traceability from the requirements in the database to the UML models and the code. So, the end users and SMEs do not see much of UML, and they are usually not asked to be able to read UML.

There are other projects where UML is starting to be the language spoken by both parties. The tool DaimlerChrysler is using in these cases is Innovator from MID, and it has allowed end users and SMEs to learn and use UML on the requirements level. However, sometimes this is just too much technical detail and the SMEs prefer to use natural speech or to draw simple pictures on a whiteboard, just not being very formal.

I think that we get the most out of MDA in the technical departments. They know about UML. The people in the IT departments are at least able to understand UML, and some of them prefer UML to informal specifications. But it really hasn't made its way down to the SMEs and end users, who talk about business processes, parts, and that kind of thing. They are not really at the level of using UML right now, and I don't think most of them will be in the near future.

On the other hand, SMEs do play a role in system design, usually not at the detailed technical level but at the system level, data flow process, data interfaces, etc. UML could be a good way to bridge these requirements with the MDA models, but very often you end up using natural speech and staying away from UML diagrams.

SMEs still prefer natural speech to UML diagrams

Summarizing, we see that UML works its way up from the detailed technical design to system landscape level, which is about how this project fits into the production environment, or how a business process interacts with other systems, et cetera. UML has not yet fully reached the specification level of SMEs.

PROCESS AND TOOLS

TSS had a sophisticated software development organization in place before they undertook the ePEP project and its model-driven approach. While they were somewhat familiar with UML and modeling, they invested in a training program in order to improve the ability of developers to work at the higher level of abstraction required by MDA.

TSS also developed their own modeling guidelines in support of their goal of achieving enterprise-wide architectural consistency. These guidelines captured their "best practice" approach to modeling a specific design pattern and its application within the system. As Thomas Maurer of Interactive Objects put it:

> Daimler was also trying to introduce company-wide architecture, including implementation guidelines, to address a problem common to many customers. They were able to extend, on their own, the patterns and "cartridges" available with our tools. This helped them to maintain their architectural standards and enforce their implementation guidelines.

Thus, for the design and implementation of the system TSS relied heavily on the ArcStyler tool and exploited its ability to customize code-generation templates. As mentioned previously, TSS was interested in improving communication between its business and IT communities. They accomplished this by modeling at a very high level of abstraction, a level at which it was possible for IT and their business counterparts to reach agreement.

We asked Wolfgang Käfer of TSS whether they found that MDA's separation of concerns made it easier or more efficient to work with the business community, and to describe the process. He said:

> We often rely on use cases to provide a better understanding of how processes interact with the system, and we use this information as a basis for talking with SMEs. So, this is more or less part of the knowledge base needed by IT to talk with SMEs, rather than documentation for the SMEs themselves. I would say that MDA improves the process, but perhaps not in a direct way.
>
> The process most often works this way: The SMEs talk to IT staff, and the result is usually a list of requirements. We formalize this list, but not always in the form of UML diagrams. There is some preliminary design in there; for example, "You should have three modules, one addressing problem area A, one area B, and so on."
>
> Validation of the requirements with the SME is done using different methods. It might be a prototype with less than full functionality. Or we might provide a presentation prototype that shows the flow of functions to the SMEs. We might talk them through use cases, and in some cases they might see UML use case diagrams, but mostly we talk them through it.

SMEs validate requirements against running prototypes, rather than against models

In this particular case, TSS then used a manual process to derive model elements at a lower level of abstraction for the PSM. This intermediate transformation was done manually because TSS felt that automated model-to-model transformation was not an important goal for them at this time.

TSS's reasoning about their use of model-to-model transformation bears examination. One factor was that they do not expect any near-term change to their PAI

Model-to-model transformation was not required because of the stability of the PAI framework…

framework, so the architectural flexibility provided by a separate PSM was not really necessary. As Wolfgang Käfer put it:

> We have the PAI framework, which is a J2EE framework that includes security, user management, and a number of other infrastructure pieces that are geared to operational scenarios at DaimlerChrysler. We do not anticipate changing this platform in the future, and it now has about 100+ applications based on it. J2EE is the strategic direction of DaimlerChrysler, so we were most concerned in aligning with PAI in this project, because it is geared toward enterprise-size projects and a complex operational environment.
>
> Given that we do not expect the platform to change, the Platform-Independent Model is not as important for us, and so we focused on other things. It might be that in another environment the PIM [Platform-Independent Model] would gain more importance but we did not see this as a risk for our project.

A second important factor was that the ArcStyler tool supports the OMG's notion of MDA notion of MDA "marks," which are lightweight platform-specific annotations to model elements. Because separate sets of marks can coexist simultaneously for a single model, and marks can easily be added or removed from a model, they do not "pollute" a PIM with platform-dependent information.

...and because ArcStyler provides an alternate OMG-supported mechanism for adding platform-specific info

We asked for clarification about how the ArcStyler tool supported the application of DaimlerChrysler's and TSS's guidelines and patterns, if that is not done in model-to-model transformations. Wolfgang Käfer said that these things were covered in the guidelines for creating models with the tool, and that the design patterns are implemented in the ArcStyler cartridges that generate code. Thomas Maurer of Interactive Objects expanded on this.

> Let me mention that our tool is unlike some others, in that we do not generate real Platform-Specific Models–because we have a highly structured Platform-Independent Model, which can be enriched with technology attributes. And so for each model element–classes, associations, methods, etc.–you assign a set of technology attributes. This set of attributes guarantees that the code generator generates the right infrastructure, and the right code in the right place.
>
> Therefore, if you start from the UML model and generate code from this for the infrastructure you do not need a real intermediate Platform-Specific Model. OMG supports both approaches: you can generate code from a true PSM or you can use what they call MDA marks to accomplish the same thing.

TSS chose Interactive Objects' ArcStyler because it provides a visual modeling environment, comprehensive code generation, and the capacity to enforce the use of architectural/design patterns as well as coding guidelines. From TSS's viewpoint, one of ArcStyler's most important features is its cartridge development environment, which supports the creation of cartridges tailored to custom architectures and custom platforms.

It should also be noted that TSS has a very process-oriented approach to developing software, and that this process mind-set aligned very well with MDA. Wolfgang Käfer said:

> DaimlerChrysler has guidelines about how to develop a software system, and it is very strict about gathering requirements before you start creating development artifacts. This has been in place for some years, and it emphasizes that you need to understand functional and nonfunctional requirements and scope before you start design and development. In our experience, this is the best way to avoid problems in the project later on.
>
> We focus on getting the requirements right, and having a good representation of the customer's requirements. Requirements management isn't just writing the requirements down and being happy when they are signed off. You really have to go back and investigate the requirements multiple times in order to make sure that we, and also the customer, have understood what the requirements mean.
>
> Going through this process costs us some time at the beginning of the project but saves a lot of time at the end. But of course this helps whether you are using MDA or a waterfall model or anything else. You can do it iteratively, as in RUP, but for each phase you need to have requirements and scope defined before you start creating things. In our case, this did not change much with the MDA approach, because we've always had the goal of getting the requirements right and then getting it into the code.

Software development guidelines focused heavily on requirements, even before MDA

We then asked about the length of the initial requirements gathering phase, and the number of people involved. Wolfgang answered:

> In our environment, the general rule is that we spend one-third of the project time on requirements gathering, and two-thirds in creation and testing. The second two-thirds might involve the iterative process of going back to the SMEs and validating requirements against delivery, as well as incorporating any changes that might have happened in the meantime.
>
> It is a rule of thumb that if you start with a development team of eight people, say, for three months, three of those people will spend those three months gathering requirements. The team is usually smaller for requirements gathering because you need to talk to SMEs in order to understand what is going on, and the number of SMEs and the time they can spend in specification is limited.
>
> It doesn't make sense to send ten people if there are only three SMEs to answer questions. But this one-third/two-thirds rule of thumb for time and budget works well for us.

The rule of thumb is that projects spend 1/3 of time and budget in requirements gathering

DIVISION OF LABOR

One of the most surprising aspects of this case study was the ratio of TSS personnel to Interactive Objects personnel on the ePEP project. Interactive Objects did not participate in the gathering of the original ePEP requirements, but they did take part in the requirements definition and evaluation of MDA for use by TSS. For this effort, Interactive Objects and TSS each provided four or five business analysts. The DaimlerChrysler participants included not only end users of the system but customers who have had problems with the system, and those involved in use case analysis as well.

DaimlerChrysler TSS personnel did the vast majority of the work

But the ratio for the development phase was much different. It involved a team of three TSS architects and three or four TSS developers at the Ulm site in Germany, and the team at the Kuala Lumpur site changed accordingly. The Kuala Lumpur team provides two architects and a team of about 14 developers who were never completely dedicated to this project.

Only one and a half Interactive Objects personnel were involved during development, and they spent most of their time at the Ulm site. The Interactive Objects consultants were more active at the beginning of the development phase, and they continue to help TSS define program checkpoints and to perform specific tasks at their request. But at no time was Interactive Objects running the project or providing a majority the human resources. As Alberto Perandones of Interactive Objects put it:

> It's sort of like teaching a kid to ride a bike—at some point you have to let them do it on their own, and that's what we have done.

MODEL DRIVEN OFFSHORING (MDO)

Another interesting aspect of this case study is the use of MDA in support of "offshoring" (or outsourcing) part of the software development effort. We saw in the DAT/GSA case study that MDA's underlying notion of "separation of concerns" fits particularly well with the federal government's development approach of using different vendors for analysis/design and implementation phases of a project. This MDA characteristic is a great advantage in offshoring as well.

Model-Driven Offshoring works where previous offshoring attempts did not

Senior managers at TSS are convinced of the advantages of offshoring. However, they had previously undertaken a project to take advantage of this approach, but it did not result in the benefits they expected. When they originally envisioned the ePEP project, the Interactive Objects team suggested that a model-driven approach might be the key to offshoring success, and indeed this has proven to be the case.

TSS's main IT center is in Ulm, Germany, where they employ architects and developers, and TSS runs an offshore site in Kuala Lumpur that provides architects as well as development staff. The cooperative development process works as follows. The TSS customer site (usually Ulm) performs high-level modeling and core design. The company uses "teamwork servers" to give their people in Germany, as well as in Kuala Lumpur, access to these models.

The Kuala Lumpur team can check out those models, work on them, and then use the ArcStyler platform to generate code (some code is hand written or generated in Ulm, but most of this work is done by Kuala Lumpur). When the Kuala Lumpur staff is finished with their work, they check the models back in and the Ulm staff goes through established procedures to ensure that the implementation is correct.

Thus, the MDA approach supports a clean handoff of specification, in the form of models, to the implementation team. In addition, the fact that TSS developed custom ArcStyler cartridges allowed them to maintain their architectural standards and enforce their implementation guidelines across both development sites.

Because Interactive Objects has extensive experience in helping their customers succeed with MDO, we asked Alberto Perandones how the process of training and transition affects the offshore organizations in the use of this approach. He said:

> The typical path is to prepare the people at the remote site; then we work together to develop a program. If they feel they have the necessary preparation and skills, they may want to do it on their own. Or they may want to make use of Interactive Objects' experience in training or project leading.
>
> If they want our help in training, we typically go there with someone from the customer's local development organization, and the training materials needed for this particular remote organization. For example, the remote site might need training in UML or in object-oriented development, or any of a number of areas needed to work in a modern development environment. So, we would tailor the training program, which might run from one to four weeks, to the needs of the remote site.
>
> Our experience is that even organizations without previous experience in UML or OO techniques can be up and running after two or three weeks. And after four to five weeks, they become productive.

We then asked about the minimum or prerequisite skill sets needed for an organization to become productive in dealing with model-based specifications. He responded:

> The minimum level is the ability to read models, to deal with information at that abstract level, and to understand the kind of information that is captured and expressed in models. Normally, in our approach there are discussions about the modeling style, the transformation logic, and the architectural blueprints.
>
> These concepts come together for the remote organization in a week, or two or three, and we ensure that they truly understand the modeling style and the transformation process. They may try to reproduce the target architecture to demonstrate their understanding to the onshore partner.
>
> There are also different kinds of offshoring partners. One kind may implement only what they get in specifications; others may verify the partner's business rules. There are now organizations in India who want to "climb up the ladder." They want to become an architecture partner as well as a development partner. We have engaged in training at various Indian companies to show them how this might work.

MDA's separation of concerns supports clean hand-offs, while tooling enforces architectural standards and coding guidelines

MDA productivity in four to five weeks

Prerequisites are the ability to read and understand models, and mastery of the target platform

But the minimum requirement is that they be able to read and understand models. And of course they need to master the target technology platform, whatever that might be.

We usually ask QSP case study participants about "Aha!" moments their clients experience during their adoption of MDA. Alberto described one such moment in the context of TSS's MDO effort.

Another Aha! moment for TSS was when they realized that the MDA approach really was going to let them work much more productively with offshore sites. The technical project leader flew down to Kuala Lumpur, and spent a week or two setting up the infrastructure for their "teamwork server" communications. The project leader sent an e-mail to the site in Germany, asking for some changes to the model.

The people in Germany did the requested work, and the Kuala Lumpur guys (led by the project leader) came to work the next morning to find the updated models. They checked out those models, saw the differences, generated the new code, and within hours they were able to test the new functionality. All they said was, "This really works!"

PROJECT EXPERIENCE

An organization that adopts MDA typically begins with a proof-of-concept project that demonstrates the approach, followed by a pilot project that provides real (and reusable) business value, followed by a full production project. In this case, TSS skipped the POC and went directly to a pilot.

The main purpose of the six-month pilot project was to build up TSS's MDA skills so that they could stand on their own feet. At the end of that pilot, the combined team stepped back and analyzed the results, benefits, and problems from both the Interactive Objects and TSS viewpoints. This resulted in modification of some processes, which were then monitored to ensure that the problems were solved. At that point, the program was expanded to include offshore sites.

The pilot project was a business investment rather than a throw-away training exercise

TSS viewed the pilot as a business investment and one of their requirements was that this investment not be thrown away. Interestingly, when we asked the Interactive Objects team about the functionality of this project they could not tell us. What they said was:

We were not really involved with the definition or development of the pilot application itself, so it's hard for us to say. Instead, we were there to help them develop the processes and transfer the knowledge needed for them to operate on their own.

We organized a team of TSS personnel such that they could modify and extend our code generators to target their own environment (the J2EE platform, in this case). But we were not involved at any point in developing the system.

ORGANIZATIONAL DEVELOPMENT

We asked Wolfgang Käfer of DaimlerChrysler TSS whether MDA is driving any changes in the organizational structure. He responded:

> Yes, we are looking at the possibility that our organization may change as a result of our MDA approach. Right now, our thinking is to have the project team work as a "silo." They will begin looking at the function that the end user wants to have, map it to the appropriate architectural level, and then start implementing it by using MDA to generate the application.
>
> Right now, each engineer on the project is aware of all the layers and has at least some basic understanding of them, and has a deeper understanding of his particular area of knowledge; for example, business logic, presentation, etc. It seems to us that we should now split the team into two groups. One team would concentrate on business logic, with a separate team (which would be shared among projects) to do technical work, concentrating on things like the persistence layer, security, etc. And of course these efforts can be cleanly separated because of the MDA approach.

Development team is split into business logic and technical infrastructure teams

RESULTS AND BENEFITS

Several case study participants mentioned that the requirements feedback loop is improved when code generation makes the feedback loop shorter. We asked Wolfgan Käfer whether his organization's experience matched this. He responded:

> From the end user's point of view, it's just a black box. They put something in, and they are happy if they get it back eight weeks later. They don't care if it is done by magic or by the addition of more software engineers. And of course in real project management you don't reduce the time by half if you double the number of people. The SMEs simply want it two months from now, and they don't care how you do it.
>
> I think that what they are seeing is that we keep the cost down, and we produce high-quality code. So, the problems that they find, and the amount of feedback they need to give to us, are less than it was before MDA.
>
> So, in general I think that is what they are seeing and how they feel about it. It is difficult to come up with numbers to describe this because it may depend on the size of the project and many other factors. But the perception is that if they get some code from us it is of high quality.

Results are difficult to quantify, but code is of high quality

We asked for a comparison of results between the old process and the MDA approach. Wolfgang answered:

> It is a tough question, and one that we have asked ourselves. The problem is that no project is the same as any other project. And if we use MDA in a project, it is very tough to try to factor out MDA.

What we can say about this MDA project is that it was done within a very complex infrastructure, and that there were many changes that had to be accommodated during the course of the project. When you take this into account, we have the feeling that we may have gained about 30% in speed of development with MDA.

We think we have improved the bug rate by 50% or perhaps 60%, as compared with the previous methodology, which involved RUP and paper specifications; that is, capturing requirements in RequisitePro repository, then giving it to the development team to implement, then giving it to the testing team for tests, and then showing it to the customers to see what they think about it.

This creates documentation as text instead of diagrams, but it is a disadvantage—if you find yourself dealing with the twentieth change request the paper specs no longer reflect the code. With the MDA approach, in this same situation our UML documentation (which is the basis of what the software engineer is doing) does match the code. So, it's a matter of speed and quality.

Also, the thinking of the development team has changed because they are forced to do the diagrams or models before they write the code. Before, they would say, "I have the diagram in my mind" when they started writing the code.

"modeling first, and then doing coding, is a much better approach"

But they didn't have that diagram as documentation. If they later provided that documentation, they might notice that some of the requirements were not addressed, and to implement those requirements at that point they had to re-factor the code. So, we think that doing the modeling first, and then doing coding, is a much better approach.

We then asked Wolfgang to describe the cultural change the team went through in adopting the new approach. He said:

It was a step-by-step process. For some of our developers this was an easy step, but for quite a number of them it was something that required a change in thinking, and that takes a while. They needed time to learn to do that smoothly, but then the benefits become apparent. I think most of our developers believe today that this is a better way to code software.

The most tangible bottom-line benefit of the Daimler TSS ePEP project was the 15% increase in development productivity they achieved, easily beating the 10% improvement they originally hoped for. They achieved their expected return on investment in less than 12 months, and they expect a total productivity increase of 30% over the course of the next year (as compared to their previous non-MDA approach).

There are intangible benefits for the development organization as well. The higher level of automation (e.g., code generation and models-as-documentation) means that local and remote developers can focus on more interesting and higher-value tasks. And the improvement in code quality—due to automation and architectural governance—mitigates project risks.

Other benefits are more difficult to measure but equally important. These include the MDA-driven optimization of a multisite development process, increased architectural and implementation consistency, better project communication/coordination, and tighter alignment of specification and code. And MDA's characteristic separation of concerns supports an efficient division of labor, which allows further optimizations.

Multisite coordination, increased consistency, and tighter alignment of specification and code...and further optimizations are in store

The architectural governance enabled by customized ArcStyler cartridges means consistent use of design patterns throughout the entire system. This in turn improves long-term maintainability of systems and applications. And the fact that Daimler TSS has chosen to maintain their models as strategic assets allows them to face the potential challenges of changing staff and changing technology platforms.

ONGOING AND PLANNED USE OF MDA

Most of DaimlerChrysler TSS's plans for MDA have to do with wringing out even more benefits from the work they have done so far. Figure 7.2 shows the current and planned levels of automation. Their MDA roadmap calls for standardization on MDA-based architecture and development, as well as quality and productivity improvements in those processes.

They also want to extend the functionality of their MDA Architecture Blueprints, and to optimize the custom ArcStyler cartridges they've developed in support of the PAI framework. Finally, they want to exploit the combination of MDA and their CMMI process framework.

But the most interesting plan for TSS's application of MDA has to do with GUIs (graphical users interfaces). In our research on various MDA projects, we found that most do not have solutions to the challenges of creating a GUI, typically because end users want their GUI to be highly customized. It may be a stylistic issue, in that they want their GUI to look a certain way, or they may have a particular concept about GUI flow or navigation. Because most MDA tools do not address these issues, an MDA project will often postpone the creation of the GUI until later in the development process.

DaimlerChrysler TSS wants to use MDA to tackle GUI development

But we discovered that Interactive Objects has a way of applying MDA to the GUI development process. Their approach is to implement the very common model-view-controller paradigm, in which each activity-diagram state is associated with a UML class. Within or associated with this UML class is a description of the GUI. The description specifies only the content of the GUI, rather than the positions of buttons, fields, or lists.

The ArcStyler tool can generate code from the models, the activity diagrams, and UML classes to create JSPs, ASP.Net artifacts, and so on. So, the same models and modeling style can be used for all supported target environments.

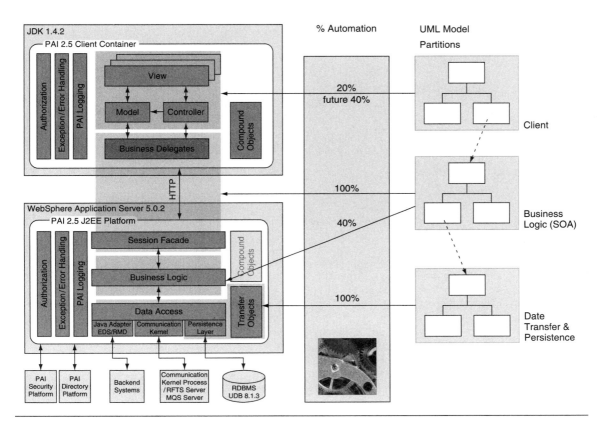

FIGURE 7.2   Current and planned levels of automation.

One of the advantages is that you can define types of GUIs. For example, you might define a GUI type that contains a list of all possible tasks on the upper half of the screen. When a user chooses a task from that list (for example, View Customer), the lower half of the screen displays the relevant information (for example, customer attributes). By defining this as a GUI type, you can reuse it. And you can specialize a GUI type with inheritance, so that it works with any kind of list (e.g., suppliers).

ArcStyler supports GUI development, and allows a generated GUI to be enhanced by other tools

ArcStyler generates the positions of the buttons and tables, and ArcStyler (like many code generation tools) supports the notion of "protected areas," which are regions that are not overwritten when code is regenerated. So, the first step captures all necessary GUI content. But at that point you can modify or redesign the layout of the GUI with another web tool, and you can preserve those modifications across new ArcStyler-driven generations of the code.

TSS has also put GUI generation on their MDA roadmap for the first half of 2006. Their first priorities were establishing the methodology for supporting their middleware and back-end frameworks, and making more profitable use of their offshore development facilities. These have been achieved.

But part of that achievement was the development of the necessary offshore skills to facilitate the next step of generating GUIs. TSS is now focusing more narrowly on this, by creating a stable and common modeling style that allows them to move to the next front-end technology with a minimum of effort.

ASSESSMENT OF THE MDA EXPERIENCE

We asked Wolfgang Käfer of DaimlerChrysler TSS about their overall assessment of the MDA experience, and whether there were any interesting "Aha!" moments he could tell us about.

I don't think we really had an "Aha!" moment. We spent 14 months investigating MDA, and saw things that worked well and things that worked not so well. But it was more of a continuous process. From the management viewpoint, after fourteen months we had a clear understanding of how MDA works, and we worked to impart that information to the team.

After that, it was a matter of continuous improvement. As you learn to use a tool, it clearly is about some particular task. Right now we have learned that re-factoring seems to be not so easy using MDA. The feeling on the team is that there must be a way to do it better. But it can be done, and we do use it that way. And in another month or two, there will be a different topic on the top of the list.

I think the next one will be the presentation layer. Right now we don't know enough about generating the presentation layer. We think it should be possible to do more, and right now the team is thinking about how to do that efficiently.

So, that is the way we approach these questions. It is not a matter of deciding at a single point in time. Dealing with MDA is a continuous process.

Developing MDA expertise is a matter of continuous improvement

We then asked, "If someone–not a competitor–came up to you and said they were interested in MDA and asked what you would advise them to do in order to get started, what would your advice be?" Wolfgang responded:

I would start by telling them to avoid looking at MDA in terms of tools. They should concentrate more on the skill level of their requirements engineers, software engineers, etc., with regard to UML, models and modeling tools, etc., and about their maturity with regard to processes.

If you develop software by putting the engineers and SMEs in the same room, then I would suggest considering organizing them in an agile way. Given that all people involved are fluent with UML, I think MDA can be a big help. I think, in such an environment I would concentrate on the tool and use this as a basis for introduction and improvement of processes. However, this is not the environment that existed for this project.

We at TSS have a strong grounding in processes, as is demonstrated by our CMMI certification. The MDA approach as provided by ArcStyler is flexible enough to conform to our processes.

TSS is focused on the development of individual software pieces in different application domains. So far, we do not see that an application-domain-specific language will help us. Consequently, we focus on the modeling- and process-related benefits of MDA.

TABLE 7.1   Project Profile: Electronic Production Planning (ePEP)

Company/Organization	*Name:* DaimlerChrysler TSS, a wholly owned subsidiary of DaimlerChrysler AG, specializing in J2EE- and .NET-based applications, Lotus Notes, and data warehousing solutions, as well as consulting and test services, all done exclusively for DaimlerChrysler AG worldwide.
	Industry/function: DaimlerChrysler AG creates products that range from small cars to sports cars to luxury sedans, and from vans to heavy trucks to coaches.
	Size: DaimlerChrysler AG has more than 38,000 employees worldwide, and revenues of more than €142.1 billion ($192.3 billion).
	Geographical reach/extent: DaimlerChrysler AG sells products in more than 200 countries.
	URL: www.daimlerchrysler.com
QSP	*Name:* Interactive Objects Software GmbH.
	Areas of experience/expertise: MDA Qualified Service Provider whose customers include many Fortune 500 companies in industries that include finance and insurance, transportation, government, software, telecommunications, and automotive.
	URL: http://www.interactive-objects.com/
Business Pain Points	The need to achieve enterprise-wide architectural consistency.
	The desire for a more successful working relationship with "offshore" (outsoure) development partners.
	The need for improved efficiency and productivity in software development.
Tools Used	Interactive Objects ArcStyler.
Model-based Artifacts Created	PIM (which was extended via ArcStyler's support for "marks," which are lightweight platform-specific annotations to model elements).

8

CHAPTER EIGHT
SUMMING UP THE PARTS

It's not obvious how to sum up the six case studies in this book. We have seen MDA used by six very different organizations, in six very different ways, to achieve six very different ends. As we mentioned in our introduction, this book is like the famous story of the blind men and the elephant: each "sees" the elephant in terms of what part he is holding. So, probably the most important point demonstrated by the six case studies in this book is that MDA, like the elephant, is far more than the simple sum of its parts.

MDA is more than the sum of its parts

An obvious corollary to this point is that MDA is also quite a bit more than any one of its parts. Unfortunately, we sometimes see articles and whitepapers that describe MDA in very one-dimensional ways, with an apparent lack of understanding of its true scope. To one "blind man" MDA is primarily about code generation; to another it means modeling everything in UML. The best way to combat this type of mischaracterization is to present real case studies, like the ones in this book, that show the many different ways in which MDA is already being profitably applied.

Because these case studies are so different from one another, we have tried to let each speak for itself as far as possible, rather than trying to shoehorn them into a single common structure. But while these case studies speak for themselves we expect that what they convey will be filtered through the individual experiences of the reader. Therefore, we will be happy if after reading this book people say, "I'm still not sure exactly what MDA is, but I find it very interesting, it seems to be applicable to some of my problems, and I want to explore it further." As in the story of the blind men, even if your perception of the MDA elephant isn't the entire picture it is still as valid as anyone else's.

MAKING THE BUSINESS CASE FOR MDA

But besides painting a broad and impressionistic picture of MDA, our purpose in writing this book is to provide some guidance to those of you who have heard of MDA, want to know more, and might be thinking of trying it out in your own organization. After all, even if we are correct in saying that MDA can be profitably applied to almost any endeavor, that doesn't by itself provide much guidance.

First of all, unless your goals are very tactical you probably hope that MDA can make some fundamental and positive changes in the way your IT organization does business, and even how your business does business. That is, there must be a business case for major transformational change. Otherwise, why bother to make the substantial investment necessary to bring in a significantly different approach? As one case study participant noted:

If there is no business case for MDA, don't bother

> The key at Harris was having a business-oriented champion who saw the value of MDA in achieving his business vision for the company. This is a company whose products are heavily dependent on software, and MDA provided a way to improve their software process and thereby improve their ability to develop products quickly.
>
> We thought that architects, developers, and all technical people would just love it. But we found that wasn't the case at all. There were many objections from the technical people; for example, the "not invented here" syndrome, or "your generated code can't possibly be as good as the code we write," etc. We found that trying to sell MDA to technologists is an uphill battle.
>
> But if you can show the business value of MDA to a businessperson in the organization, and they sponsor MDA, the technology people will grudgingly get on board. And once they get on board, the technologists often say, "This is great stuff!"

At GSA, the approach was similar.

> In the development of the OneGSA project, we spent a lot of time with the finance group doing preliminary work at the business level. They began to see MDA's capabilities, and they ended up funding this finance project (jointly with the OCIO).

Today, it is an emerging consensus that every business needs to continuously adapt to changing conditions merely to survive, and certainly to gain competitive advantage. Further, IT can be viewed as a special case in that it has to both help its business clients adapt to change and simultaneously adapt itself to the rapid change inherent in the IT industry itself.

IT is a special case when it comes to adapting to change

Certainly the participants in each of our case studies have understood the need for this type of change in both the business and IT. However, as those case studies also make clear, an organization's basic characteristics—strengths, weaknesses, expertise, and culture—can significantly affect how MDA is used and adopted by an enterprise. Often this can make it difficult to predict a priori exactly how MDA will end up working in your organization. In many ways, the journey to MDA may well end up changing the goals as much as the goals end up guiding the journey.

But as we just noted, nobody is going to make a major investment in any new and transformational approach unless they can first make a decent business case for trying it out. The usual approach to establishing a business case for a new approach is to try to show how it can make development–and maintenance–"better, faster, cheaper." For the most part, however, this just begs the issue, because you can only achieve "better, faster, cheaper" with any new approach by identifying the various ways in which you intend to apply that approach to specific projects in your particular organization.

Business "pain points" that are amenable to an MDA approach

That is, as our case studies very clearly indicate, there is no "one size fits all" business case to be made for MDA. In addition, it is well beyond the scope of this book to provide a "how-to" methodology for building a detailed business case for MDA. That said, in the interest of helping our readers find a starting point for developing their own business case, we have identified the following (nonexhaustive) list of common high-level problem areas (or "pain points") MDA can very effectively be used to address, and which have been reasonably well illustrated in our six case studies. Some of these areas may overlap, but each emphasizes a distinct focus for making a business case, and may provide some food for further thought.

- *Separation of concerns:* Projects that need to enforce a clear "separation of concerns" among the various types of participants
- *Traceability:* Projects where traceability of requirements to implementation and deployment is absolutely necessary, or is mandated by corporate or regulatory imperatives
- *Stakeholder communication:* Projects that typically involve many large and/or varied stakeholder communities who must communicate effectively
- *Agile and iterative development:* Projects that want, need, or are mandated to introduce a more agile and iterative development process

Each of these topics could probably justify at least a chapter of explanation by itself. However, let's now take a very brief look at each of them.

SEPARATION OF CONCERNS

Many organizations require a software development process in which there is a very clear separation of concerns between different participants, while still maintaining overall coordination. This may be due to a variety of factors, including the need to hide certain information from some participants (for example, in the military) or the need to cleanly divide up work among different teams in different locales, as in offshoring (outsourcing). In this case, each team needs to see only the information they require, but in a form most conducive to their assigned task.

Using MDA, it is possible to create distinct "viewpoints" that provide each group of participants with only the information they need, while keeping all of the information across a project in synch. For example, business people typically need to see one viewpoint (for example, computation-independent business process models, or CIMs), analysts another viewpoint (for example, platform-independent analysis models, PIMs), and developers need to see yet another (for example, platform-specific design models, PSMs). Using MDA, it is also possible to create more fine-grained viewpoints, similar to the blueprints used to construct a building. At the GSA, separation of concerns and division of labor were paramount.

Viewpoints filter information as appropriate for stakeholders, and allow information to remain in synch across the project

> All along, GSA had the vision and the desire to use MDA to separate concerns, to allow the business to drive the technology, and to allow the business to take advantage of technology changes when they happen. So, the whole concept of separation of concerns was a driving force. We are starting to get to the realization of this vision in the finance drill-down project.
>
> This is why MDA's separation of concerns is of such great value when working with the federal government. If you want to do such work, and you must separate the implementation details from the specification (and you usually do), this is a fine way to go about it.
>
> The reason for these rules is to prevent a large system integrator from creating a specification that only they can implement. So, in a very real sense MDA is an enabler for companies that want to participate in this business. And it illustrates the fact that separation of concerns is not simply something of abstract interest in the IT organization.
>
> Here, it is a necessity from the business viewpoint. So, MDA is a powerful enabler in a very large business segment—the federal government. And as GSA goes so will go much of the national government, and many local governments and quasi-public organizations as well.

In this case, a specific form of "separation of concerns" is required by policies that mandate that different organizations be responsible for the different stages of any given project. For example, according to GSA regulations the contractor who specifies a solution can't be the same one who implements it.

Therefore, GSA is using MDA to precisely define what must be modeled in each viewpoint, so that it can properly control the flow of information to and from the different participants throughout the solution creation process. GSA also hopes to gain many other advantages from MDA, but this is probably the most obvious and compelling business driver for justifying their investment in a new approach.

By precisely modeling the content of each viewpoint, the flow of information among participants can be controlled

> By modeling the processes at the level of roles, collaborations, activities, and subactivities you reach a level where you can very precisely describe what is going on in the business environment. People can see the roles they'll be playing as well as the

Viewpoints clarify the relationships between development artifacts

relationship between systems and people. For example, at the CIM level we modeled the value chain processes irrespective of whether they are implemented in systems or by people.

While GSA could have done the "to be" modeling in other ways, the value here is that it could immediately be used to drive the next step of defining the system. MDA allowed us to reach the level of precision needed to take the models to the next step, down to the PIM, and enabled the development of specifications for the next level of system detail.

The point of all this is that with the MDA paradigm you must express the very detailed level of precision needed to take it to the next level of detail. For example, as we develop the PIM we may find that we have to go back and revise the CIM because we have not been precise enough.

At the Austrian Health Service, the separation of concerns that MDA enforces has had the following impact.

I think the relationship between the different artifacts, at different levels, is clearer with MDA, and the clarity of these relationships may make it easier. So, while there might be some difficulties in terms of where to put information (for example, sometimes there might be too much technical detail at too high a level) this is a problem that we've had in the past, so these are typical problems not MDA problems.

The relationship between the different levels is clearer now because it is clearly defined in terms of how to transform from one to another. If you do this by hand, it is possible to violate those relationships and cause confusion. So, in this regard it is easier for people to see what belongs in one model versus another, and how these models relate to one another.

At DaimlerChrysler, there is a similar need to clearly enforce separation of concerns, in this case to enable reliable offshoring. It was already obvious to Daimler that offshoring had the potential to significantly reduce development costs, and equally obvious that earlier attempts to get a successful result from offshoring had largely failed.

Another "Aha!" moment for Daimler was when they realized that the MDA approach really was going to let them work much more productively with offshore sites. The technical project leader flew down to Kuala Lumpur and spent a week or two there setting up the infrastructure for their "teamwork server" communications. The project leader sent an e-mail to the site in Germany, asking for some changes to the model. The people in Germany did the requested work, and the Kuala Lumpur guys (led by the project leader) came to work the next morning to find the updated models. They checked out those models, saw the differences, generated the new code, and within hours they were able to test the new functionality. All they said was, "This really works!"

MDA helps control the division of labor and enforces architectural constraints

So, MDA has provided a way for Daimler to clearly delineate what information had to be collected by analysts at the front end of a project in order to provide a complete and precise set of specifications sufficient to guide an offshore software implementation team on the other side of globe. It also provided a way to ensure that the results of the offshore team would meet the architectural constraints of Daimler's target environment. Once again, Daimler expects to get other advantages from MDA, but supporting a clear division of labor between their different teams was by itself more than enough to justify investing in a new approach.

> Right now, each engineer on the project is aware of all the layers and has at least some basic understanding of them, and has a deeper understanding of his particular area of knowledge; for example, business logic, presentation, etc. It seems to us that we should now split the team into two groups. One team would concentrate on business logic, with a separate team (which would be shared among projects) to do technical work (concentrating on things like the persistence layer, security, etc.). And of course these efforts can be cleanly separated because of the MDA approach.

At Coopservice, the need for clear separation of concerns may be an even more compelling business requirement. For each contract, Coopservice must orchestrate the various IT systems of its participating members. It must therefore maintain a clear distinction between its core business model, which is a kind of B2B backbone, and the various member-owned systems that plug into it.

> The main reason we chose an MDA approach for Coopservice was the ability to model the business—for example, business processes—in a way that did not depend on the technology platform or computing techniques. We pursue service contracts with enterprises on a competitive basis. But we offer services from a network of companies, and these companies collaborate to fulfill those service contracts. The B2B capability makes it easier for us to define and deliver that solution because it works with all the IT systems that individual cooperating companies use. These cooperating partners find it easier to work with us than with competing prime contractors, and that is a business advantage for us.

TRACEABILITY AND GOVERNANCE

Many organizations have bemoaned the difficulties of maintaining a clear link between the business requirements specified for a given system and the resulting implementation. This most common problem is to figure out some way to make sure that the stated requirements are actually realized in the application. This is a big issue not only for development per se but for governance. At GSA:

> We have experienced the classic gap, where the business people come in and say that there is something you need to do that doesn't map to your organization. Then architects come in and design a system and hand it over to coders. Basically, everyone

ignores what the guy further up the chain has said. So, the explicit traceability that is part of the central MDA message, as you walk from one abstraction to another, or to some concrete artifact, is very attractive to us.

Traceability can tell you the business impact of a component failure

Just as importantly, if a requirement changes (either during development or later on to support maintenance or enhancements) it can be quite useful to know exactly what parts of the implementation will have to be altered. A related issue, often overlooked, is that in the event of a failure of an implementation component subsequent to its deployment it may be valuable to be able to trace back to requirements in order to figure out which critical functions of the business may be impacted. In other words, if server X or module Y fails you need to know exactly what part of the business may go down with it. At the Austrian Health Service:

> With respect to maintenance, I think that that is a function of the specific changes that are required over the course of the application's lifetime. MDA is a methodology very well suited to this, because the changes can be specified at a high level, and it is clear how the change will manifest itself in the code.
>
> Most of the coding details are fixed as a result of the business logic being specified. So, for maintenance MDA is a very good thing because the patterns in use are always the same and are used in the same way. So, if you see a pattern in one place you can be sure the pattern is used the same way throughout the application.
>
> Of course, developers have always tried to encourage this kind of uniformity in usage, but in practice there were always slight differences. And this often caused problems, because the people who make the changes usually know only one way in which a pattern is used, and are not familiar with all the variants. I think this is the greatest MDA advantage in terms of maintenance.

These thoughts were basically echoed (by Alberto Perandones of Interactive Objects) in the context of the DaimlerChrysler TSS project.

> While you can suggest to the customer that MDA benefits productivity in software development, some studies suggest that eighty percent of the IT budget typically goes toward maintenance of existing systems. Note that maintenance is part of the "strategic" budget because it governs the operation of systems in support of business, whereas the development budget is not strategic. If you can demonstrate that MDA can influence this strategic maintenance budget, then you have access to the people who control that budget—and this can result in many new project opportunities.

Although maintaining some level of traceability has always been deemed "best practice" for software development, only recently has it become a compelling business need and only in a few highly regulated industries (such as the military and aerospace) where system failures may have obvious life-and-death consequences.

However, with the coming of broader regulatory laws (such as Sarbanes-Oxley) traceability and governance are becoming increasingly hot issues everywhere. Sarbanes-Oxley and Gramm-Leach-Bliley in the United States, and The Corporations Law Economic Reform Policy in Australia, now actually impose serious penalties for executives whose companies fail to demonstrate that they are complying with certain government regulations.

Today's regulatory environment makes traceability essential

In general, MDA addresses the problem of traceability by formally specifying the transformations between different steps in the development process, from requirements gathering to deployment. Depending on how rigorously this notion is applied throughout the development process, it should then be possible to examine any artifact generated during that process and trace backward to the originating requirements, or forward to the resulting deployed components. For more examples from our case studies, we can again look to GSA and their "line of sight" requirement, as well as their stated desire to trace performance metrics to actual business outcomes.

And a very important point here is that the traceability inherent in the MDA approach is a big advantage. When you are working with the PIM, the trace between function and implementation is much clearer than was the case with traditional analysis methods. MDA gives you the ability—it almost forces you—to provide the FEA-mandated "line of sight" visibility between requirements and implementation.

The theme here is that we have the ability to remodel a very large enterprise in a way that lets you achieve these downstream results with traceability. This is perhaps the most valuable and the most extraordinary result of these projects.

The Harris and DaimlerChrysler studies also noted the importance of traceability as a way of controlling the change management process during development, and in subsequent maintenance and upgrades. At Harris:

The benefit of this was that as soon as you understand how the software is to be organized and structured in one part, you know it will be organized and structured in the same way in all parts. This meant that someone working on one part of the project could quickly move to another part and be productive immediately.

Ensuring consistency via tools is better than relying on the self-discipline of developers...

Harris specifically said that this consistency helped them accomplish integration. As they were taking our software and integrating it into their existing environment, they felt that this consistency made integration a lot easier. Of course, this also helps reinforce the consistent application of design patterns and software best practices by the team, and this consistency was also evident throughout the application.

Finally, the quick feedback loop in the process of turning requirements into production software was also an important realization. Anyone involved in requirements specification could quickly see how well the implementation fulfilled that specification.

In many cases with other approaches to requirements capture, it takes a long time to see the impact of what you have done. In this case, we were able to shorten that cycle to a degree that people came to understand how important it was to have

...and a short feedback cycle for requirement validation is much better than a long one

high-quality requirements. This was a real learning experience for the requirements analysts, and its success encouraged business users to become much more involved in the software development process.

At Coopservice, using MDA to enforce governance was actually a stated goal.

The implementation of a governance layer was always a main goal of the project. However, there were many other challenges we had to face before addressing that one, and we thought that we would not be able implement a governance layer until late in 2006. But after four or five months of experience with MDA tools and associated processes we found that it was much easier to do the governance layer than we thought it would be.

A part of this governance layer is already in place. We have implemented a "governance cockpit" that allows real-time monitoring of business processes, and also provides controls for modifying these processes, even if they span business units within Coopservice. These process modifications do not require coding, deployment, or system updates. Thus, at Coopservice governance is not simply portfolio management; it is business process management.

OMG is developing standards for regulatory compliance models

It is also interesting to note that as a further extension of its MDA activities the OMG itself has recently launched some new initiatives to address traceability and governance issues related to government regulation. The OMG Regulatory Compliance SIG is in the process of developing standards for models that support regulatory compliance in business processes, and the OMG plans to develop a global repository (available exclusively to OMG members) of regulations that have a significant impact on IT.

STAKEHOLDER COMMUNICATION

Most organizations would agree that, during a software development project, maintaining good communication among the various stakeholders is a key success factor. Poor communications can plague different groups that need to collaborate even within a single IT department. However, it is typically even worse when we are considering the relationship between groups that have significantly different frames of reference, such as between the IT and its business clients. It is no secret that dysfunctional IT/business communication is one of the most common and vexing problem areas in a wide range of enterprises.

Good communication means keeping stakeholders in the loop without wasting their time

But what do we really mean by "good communications"? On the one hand, key business decision makers not only need to be constructively engaged during requirements gathering, but they also need to be kept in the loop during development–especially in that requirements may change or the proper interpretation of the requirements may not be clear. At the same time, such communication must be efficient, as it is counterproductive to monopolize stakeholders' time. Obviously, sending the business reams of artifacts full of IT jargon at each stage of development is hardly the proper approach. At the Austrian Health Service:

> As is the case for many of our clients, some of the straight UML models became too abstract and "too logical" for the designers to find much value in them, or they became "too physical" in nature and therefore became incomprehensible to the analysts. So, there was a semantic mismatch between these two teams, and that is certainly one of the reasons why Hauptverband felt that MDA was the right approach for them: the fact that they could, first, separate out those abstractions to the benefit of the longevity of project and solution, and second, express their best practices in terms of architectural design patterns and apply them in the transformation between the PIM and PSM.
>
> So, that was a key driver for them, and I believe they are realizing that benefit. Certainly within the project team that is true.

The same project also used MDA as a communication enabler between the architects and developers.

> The first benefit was better communication between the architecture team and the project team. Before, the project team was not really following the instructions about the technical implementation. In some cases, it was because they did not want to follow such strict rules, and in other cases there were simply misunderstandings.
>
> But this project demonstrated clearly how the technical architecture should be used, as well as the mapping between PIM and PSM. That made the technical architecture much more pure.
>
> It also meant that people who were new to the project were able to use these templates to gain a deeper understanding of the technical architecture, and that saved a lot of time. They were able to take part in the project much sooner than originally estimated.

Structured communication improves architectural compliance and time-to-productivity for participants

In every one of our case studies, the participants reported that the introduction of MDA resulted in some form of significant improvement in stakeholder communications, particularly between the business and IT. According to one of the participants at Ohio JFS:

> So, there was a constant, and short, feedback loop between the developers and the business stakeholders. It was not at all like the old approach where you develop for eighteen months behind closed doors and roll out the result only then for user approval. There was constant checking with the business.

Obviously, we can't claim that MDA by itself is wholly responsible for this improvement, since there are many organizational and cultural factors that determine how well different groups in a given organization or cross-organizational project communicate. It may even be argued that organizations likely to be receptive to MDA are exactly those already taking other steps to improve communication among stakeholders. However, it should also be clear that the MDA approach allows each type of stakeholder to maintain his own culture-specific "viewpoint" while remaining in good coordination and communication with other types of stakeholders.

"Culture-specific" viewpoints make it easier to determine the impact of change

For example, should a business requirement change subsequent to system design or even implementation, MDA should make it much easier to figure out which system components are likely to be impacted as compared with using traditional development methods. Similarly, it should be much easier to figure out how a given set of implementation options ties back to the original business requirements, and to communicate the likely impact of these options to the business in their own vernacular. Coopservice describes exactly how it was able to manage its communication with the business on such matters.

> We talked with the business community about dependencies between components, use cases, business object models, business processes, business events, and so on. But we did not discuss computation-specific issues such as interfaces or exceptions.

At Harris:

Letting business people clearly see where requirements lead results in more support for the delivered solution

> The MDA approach we used helped improve communication and understanding between the business and IT communities in several ways. We captured requirements with use cases. We built a PIM that was separate from any implementation details. We focused on business entities and their relationships in the PIM and through those models, which gave the team a good perspective of the business aspects.
>
> But there was also the fact we were able to take use cases and using our MDA Express tool quickly generate working software that they could use to validate the accuracy of the requirements. So, they could see these models in what could be described as executable form and very quickly correct them.
>
> There is also an interesting effect, in that the business people were able to be part of the process in a new way. They were used to gathering requirements, but in this case they were also brought in and shown what those requirements led to. This helped garner support for the solution that was finally delivered.
>
> The business people were intimately involved and had a feedback mechanism as we built the models during the various iterations. That improved communication with the business community and it meant that they knew what they were getting before it was delivered. They were ready for it and already happy with what they were going to get.

As we just noted, all of the case studies demonstrate the ability of MDA to improve communication among stakeholder communities, and especially between business and IT. But this capability was particularly evident in the Ohio JFS and U.S. GSA case studies, in which the inclusion of many communities is mandated and in which the set of stakeholders and other interested parties is large. To put it another way, the more ducks you have to line up the more you need MDA.

More specifically, the GSA case study identified business process modeling/management as a potential MDA "sweet spot," and demonstrated the importance of MDA as a way of structuring business processes defined in terms of roles, conversations, and so on.

> As for the help MDA provided in this communication, once we got people into the room together the models themselves readily facilitated communication and discussion. We had a number of lengthy intense sessions about the validity of the models. So, the models provided the key tool to describe the desired to-be state of the business, and for enabling the business people to understand this state.

AGILE AND ITERATIVE DEVELOPMENT

For some time, a movement has been afoot to liberate IT from what are perceived to be rigid and cumbersome "waterfall" development methodologies, and to adopt approaches that are more agile and iterative. Although these terms are relative and clearly open to wide interpretation, it is interesting that nearly all case study participants agreed with these goals and felt that MDA has in this respect been a major enabler in achieving them.

In contrast to conventional wisdom, MDA practitioners think that MDA is an enabler for agile software development

What makes MDA agile, or at least an enabler of "agile"? According to our case study participants at the Ohio JFS and Harris, automatic code generation shortened the time required to complete development iterations, thereby enabling more iterations and a more active feedback loop by which business SMEs could validate that requirements had been met. In both cases, the use of MDA-style code generation also ensured architectural conformance, which greatly simplified and accelerated testing and integration.

The consensus from our case studies is that approximately 15 to 40% of system code—largely business logic and algorithms—is really interesting to developers, while the rest is error-prone drudgery. Using MDA to automate the drudgery allowed developers to concentrate on the interesting parts, which also corresponded to those areas of prime interest to the business. In the eyes of the business, this made the developers more agile. According to Ohio JFS:

More interesting development work, less error-prone drudgery

> But note that the agile development took place in the business logic implemented by individual developers. As you build out the business logic, and do the development work that cannot be automated, that is where you employ agile process at the development level. But at the architectural level you have the rigor and control, as well as the metrics needed by management.
>
> This project almost looks like the old waterfall methodology, but when you get down to the implementation of a business use case by a programmer you see the agile development processes: working in small teams, paired programming, collaboration,

quick iterations, face-to-face meetings, and all the tenets of agile programming. But this is part of the larger framework that offers management what they need as well.

And

"Agile MDA" lets you pick your development battles

In a sense, this eight-five/fifteen split actually allows agile programming to be used for large projects–but where it is appropriate rather than everywhere. I think the agile methodologies are very good for small teams and small projects (five to eight people). In that situation, you might not need the rigor that MDA brings. But if you want to build an enterprise system that involves the interrelations and complexities of a statewide child welfare system this is the way to enable agile methods to work on a large project.

At Harris, MDA was used to focus scarce resources on the most important areas.

Our vision was based on the 80/20 "Pareto principle." If I could get them to produce 80% of the low-level code–kind of the horsepower under the hood–while I spend my effort, time, and resources focused on the domain of the application (that is, specifying the requirements the application must meet to satisfy my customers) then so much the better.

And I think that any program manager in the world who has budget and time constraints, and is looking for ways to mitigate risk, can use MDA as a method that allows them to identify and stay focused on that twenty percent of capabilities that really satisfy their customers' requirements.

In the final analysis, "agile" means responding more quickly to customer demand

For Coopservice, the agile nature of MDA has been manifested in a completely different and rather novel way: MDA allows Coopservice to more rapidly configure an accurate bid in response to customer requests. This really goes to the heart of "agile"–the ability to respond quickly to customer requests. Coopservice sees MDA as an enabler to landing more business.

As a company, we offer service solutions in the areas of cleaning, security, and industrial processes. The delivery of these solutions requires the cooperation of other companies. MDA allowed us to change our approach to the realization and delivery of the solution, to the economic benefit of our customers.

We need to be able to dynamically change the process by which we connect with our partners, and in order to do that we need a software development and deployment approach that allows us to respond much more quickly. We pursue service contracts with enterprises on a competitive basis. But we offer services from a network of companies, and these companies collaborate to fulfill those service contracts. The B2B capability makes it easier for us to define and deliver that solution because it works with all the IT systems that individual cooperating companies use. These cooperating partners find it easier to work with us than with competing "prime contractors," and that is a business advantage for us.

And finally, at the Austrian Health Service:

This customer is working with large teams, and with external contractors. So, although they want to be agile they also want to be in control of things. I think the MDA approach satisfies both those objectives. With automated code generation they can get the right level of control over productivity and best practices–by exploiting MDA's separation of concerns and by applying patterns, which takes them right down to the code level.

That gives them a quick approach to their code base, and of course it can quickly change things in them. The ability to control the transformation of models means that they can control their implementation artifacts. This fits with the level of rigor they want, as well as the agility and productivity they want from an agile approach. So, I think MDA and agile development are complementary rather than in opposition.

THE OMG'S FASTSTART PROGRAM

The MDA FastStart program is managed by the OMG[1] to help IT organizations learn about MDA and to apply MDA to their systems architecture, systems integration, and software development activities. MDA FastStart is the quickest way to learn how to use MDA, and you don't have to be an OMG member to take advantage of this program.

As its name implies, MDA FastStart is designed to familiarize information technology organizations with MDA concepts and to start integrating MDA into their mission-critical software development activities. During a FastStart engagement, highly qualified OMG-endorsed consultants and trainers provide an integrated set of assessment, planning, executive seminar, and technical practicum activities targeted to both top executives and technical staff. FastStart deliverables allow key decision makers to:

- Clearly analyze and plan how MDA can best be introduced and applied to most benefit their organization and its key business drivers
- Decisively demonstrate how MDA can provide clear-cut business value sufficient to justify further investment in MDA-related activities
- Attain sufficient knowledge of MDA to confidently initiate further MDA-related activities, with or without the further assistance of external service providers

---

1　More specifically, it is managed by Michael K. Guttman, one of the authors of this book.

MDA FastStart includes assessment, planning, executive seminar, and technical practicum activities that can be delivered in a relatively short period (typically 5 to 10 weeks, depending on the specific organization). If required, additional units of customized consulting and mentoring services are available.

MDA FASTSTART ACTIVITIES AND DELIVERABLES

MDA FastStart includes the following categories of activities.

- MDA Readiness Assessment
- MDA Enterprise Architecture Review
- MDA Transition Plan
- MDA Executive Seminars
- MDA Practicum

MDA FASTSTART ASSESSMENT

The FastStart assessment is used to determine the best overall approach to introducing MDA into the organization. It includes the following activities.

- A high-level review of the business drivers relevant to introducing MDA, and identification of target technical activities best suited to those business drivers
- A high-level review of the various technological drivers and tools in the organization that would influence MDA transition, including current software development processes and related computing infrastructure
- A high-level review by FastStart consultants of the organizational scope, size, and structure of the target MDA users, as well as the human resources available to support MDA activities

The primary assessment deliverable is a brief report with recommendations for presentation to customer management. In addition, information gathered during the period of the assessment is used to scope and customize the subsequent FastStart activities.

MDA ENTERPRISE ARCHITECTURE REVIEW

The architecture review is used to determine in more detail the technical specifics of the organization's current architectural foundation, including the following.

- The level of maturity associated with current enterprise/application architecture efforts
- What parts of the enterprise architecture and computing infrastructure offer the most beneficial and cost-effective focal points for future MDA-related efforts
- How MDA can best be adapted to the architectural paradigms currently in use

These and related matters are summarized in a brief report (with recommendations) to be presented to technical management. In addition, this information is used to better focus subsequent FastStart activities.

MDA TRANSITION PLAN

The transition plan is a set of recommendations and a high-level plan for introducing and incorporating MDA into the customer's organization. It is based on MDA best practices and the results of the assessment and architecture review. It includes the selection of a set of specific technical activities for the MDA Practicum activity and an evaluation of the various modeling and MDA tools appropriate to the customer's organization and technical requirements.

MDA EXECUTIVE SEMINARS

The seminars provide a variety of options customized as appropriate to each organization. Typically, this includes the following.

- A half-day Executive Seminar aimed at business and IT management. This seminar describes the overall ideas around MDA and explains the benefits, requirements, and timeframe of implementing an MDA transition program in the specific organization. The Executive Seminar also includes the presentation of the Assessment and Architecture Review reports and recommendations, as well as the proposed Transition Plan.
- A one-day Technical Seminar aimed at architects, designers, modelers, and engineering managers to discuss the principles, techniques, tools, and so on involved in implementing MDA.

MDA PRACTICUM

The practicum is a highly interactive two-week activity aimed at senior technical staff, such as enterprise and system architects, designers, and project managers. It includes formal detailed presentations on MDA technology topics and a set of workshop periods that allow the participants to apply what they learn in a pragmatic fashion. The practicum is typically scheduled to minimize any disruption of daily activities.

The practicum includes a client-specific project that has been selected through the Assessment and Architecture Review activities and that allows participants to apply MDA skills to actual development efforts for their company. Practicum participants are typically limited to ensure maximum interaction between the practicum leader and the participants. Participants work as individuals and as a team at various points during the workshop.

APPENDIX

A (VERY) BRIEF MDA PRIMER

This primer is intended to provide the readers of the book with a short and very basic understanding of the fundamentals of MDA, for the purpose of better appreciating the book's six case studies. It is not intended to substitute for the many excellent books and articles that cover MDA and related topics much more exhaustively. For those who may wish to read further on this subject, we've included a few of these publications in a short "Further Reading" section at the end of this primer.

WHAT IS MDA?

MDA–Model Driven Architecture–is trademark of the Object Management Group (OMG), a 500+ member international software industry consortium, which also owns and controls related modeling standards such as the Unified Modeling Language (UML), and, more recently, the Business Process Modeling Notation (BPMN). At the OMG, MDA is used as umbrella acronym for a broad set of modeling-related concepts, standards and practices that include UML and BPMN, but goes well beyond them.

Besides the acronym MDA, you have probably heard a lot recently about "model-driven development" (sometimes abbreviated as MDD), model-driven software development (MDSD), agile model driven development (AMDD), "software factory," and many other variants, with even more on the way. Strictly speaking, these somewhat related non-OMG terms are not necessarily MDA, although some may be specialized applications of MDA. In any case, they do indicate that the model-driven approach to software engineering that MDA has pioneered is gaining considerable market momentum and legitimacy–after all, imitation is the sincerest form of flattery!

On the other hand, all the market-babble about "model-driven" can become confusing, and, without some foundational concepts, ultimately the term may start to seem meaningless. So, let's take a step back and discuss what the real (OMG) MDA is, where it came from, and where it is going. Once we do, it should become a bit clearer where some of the variants fit in, and also how MDA fits with other approaches to software architecture.

IN THE BEGINNING ...

MDA emerged initially because of the growing popularity of OMG's Unified Modeling Language (UML). In 1997, the OMG issued UML as a general-purpose modeling standard to replace a plethora of different, but function-ally similar, object-oriented modeling languages–Booch, Rumbaugh, Jacobsen, Schlerer-Meilor, etc. The result was a huge success, and today UML is the clear market leader in this space.

Subsequently, the commercial use of UML–and formal modeling in general–broadened and deepened considerably. Originally, UML was focused primarily on modeling the object-oriented structure of a single application–a kind of specialized data modeling language. But over time UML has increasingly come to be used to model many more aspects of the software environment–business use cases, activity flows, logical constraints, state machines, patterns, deployment packaging, component architectures, etc.

Of course, that was great news to UML vendors and their loyal customers. However, as is usually the case, the success of UML brought up a whole new set of issues. Perhaps the most vexing ones were: (1) how to organize all those models into a coherent overall architecture, and (2) how to use that architec-ture to control the overall modeling process. And that's exactly where MDA comes in.

When MDA was introduced in 2002, it was primarily intended to help organize the otherwise infinite number of possible modeling approaches into a coherent framework. Using MDA, formal models could be used not only to help describe individual systems, but even complex webs of related applications and supporting services. To the modeling mavens at OMG, the end result would be a formally specified "model-driven architecture," an approach that could be applied to almost any software engineering domain.

By the way, you may have noticed that, in the last paragraph, I stopped referring to UML specifically, and shifted to discussing modeling in general. That's because, as it has evolved, MDA is no longer 'dependent' specifically on UML. Yes, MDA may have 'born' out of UML, but it didn't take long before it branched out to be modeling-language-agnostic. We'll discuss this key point in more detail a little later on.

A SEPARATION OF CONCERNS

In any case, MDA was initially intended to help modeling practitioners get a better grip on how to use formal modeling in a much broader context. To do so, MDA leveraged a well-known architectural approach commonly called 'separation of concerns.'

In terms of MDA, this essentially means structuring models so that, for example, the elements used to model business entities like 'customer' or 'account' are clearly separated from the elements used to describe implementation details, such as 'database' or 'message protocol.' This allows business analysts to focus on modeling business logic, without having to be 'concerned' with system-level details, which can be dealt with 'separately' by system analysts and developers.

To achieve this separation of concerns, MDA defines different 'viewpoints,' each of which shows only the model elements associated with a given 'area of concern.' The OMG's MDA Guide specifically defines three high-level viewpoints—the Computation-Independent Model (CIM), the Platform-Independent Model (PIM), and the Platform-Specific Model (PSM). In this context the use of the term 'model' (instead of 'viewpoint') can be confusing, since there is really just one integrated model, which is then selectively presented to different audiences, each with its own viewpoint.

In any case, the CIM viewpoint is supposed to include only the model elements necessary to describe the functional problem domain from a business viewpoint, and is therefore developed primarily by business analysts. The PIM viewpoint, developed by system analysts, then includes additional model elements to describe the computational logic necessary to realize the CIM functionality, but without implementation platform specifics.

Finally, the PSM viewpoint, developed by system designers, provides additional model elements that describe exactly how to realize the CIM and PIM elements in a specific target environment ('platform')—for example, Java with EJB, or C# with .NET, or even COBOL with DB2. A very common application of the PSM is to use it to automatically generate code and other implementation and deployment artifacts for the target platforms.

It's important to remember that there is nothing sacred to MDA about the CIM-PIM-PSM pattern—it's just one convenient way of dividing up all the possible viewpoints at a very high level. Using MDA, even the CIM, PIM, and PSM can be broken down into sub-viewpoints, all of which conceptually still embody one unified (or federated) model. The important point of the CIM-PIM-PSM pattern is that provides a way of conceptualizing the main areas of 'separation of concerns.'

We should note that you can also use MDA to create other viewpoints, some of which may cross the CIM-PIM-PSM viewpoint boundaries. For example, we can create a set of viewpoints based on various functional roles, such as business analysts, system analysts, architects, project manager, etc. Many of these role-based viewpoints might cross several or all the standard CIM-PIM-PSM viewpoints. The good news is that MDA doesn't really care—it is happy to support any number of viewpoints and viewpoint patterns, even if they overlap.

Of course it is very often quite convenient to standardize on at least some of these viewpoints. But, as we shall shortly see, the real value in MDA is that it allows us to define—and refine—those viewpoints, and all the associated modeling languages, notations and artifacts, in a standard way. The net result is that the different viewpoints integrate with each other, and can readily exchange common model information as needed.

By the way, many books and articles about MDA make a big deal about how MDA tools can be used to generate code automatically from a properly constructed PSM, and sometimes even to generate a PSM automatically from a PIM. There's no doubt that using MDA in this way can save lots of time and effort otherwise spent in hand coding and associated debugging. But it should already be clear from our description that this is only one possible use of MDA, and not nearly the whole picture. We'll make this even clearer in a moment.

THE BACKBONE OF MDA

As the early proponents of MDA went down the original CIM-PIM-PSM route, it soon became clear that it was not going to be enough to describe all possible viewpoints in UML, or any other single specific modeling language, for that matter. Sure, maybe the UML standard could eventually be extended to cover the whole waterfront of software development, but that was probably not a realistic approach for at least a decade or two, and maybe never.

The problem with focusing exclusively on UML, or any one notation/language is that there are already any number of other popular notations, standards with supporting products for modeling data structures, message protocols, business processes, and so on, with more coming out all the time. That also means there are a lot of vendors, consultants and end-users using those non-UML notations and associated tools, most of whom have no obvious incentive to switch to a different modeling language just to become 'UML-compliant.' It's pretty obvious that UML would be very unlikely to supplant all of them any time soon, no matter how much it was extended.

So, it soon became clear to MDA advocates that MDA would have to find a way to integrate languages and tools other than those based on UML into the MDA vision, even where OMG had no direct control over that integration. Therefore, the OMG adapted another of its existing standards, the Meta Object Facility (MOF), to serve this purpose for MDA. In so doing, MOF essentially became the real backbone of MDA.

So, what is the MOF? The MOF is itself a modeling language, but one used specifically to formally model other modeling languages, for example, the OMG's own UML and BPMN. The idea of MOF is to capture the underlying elements of each modeling language using the same basic constructs. (For those who like to think this way, MOF is a meta-meta language used to model the meta-models of other languages.)

The beauty of MOF is that it makes it much easier for different tools to exchange and coordinate modeling information across different models, different kinds of models, and different modeling tools. The only really critical requirement is that the modeling languages involved are themselves modeled in MOF.

Now, it's easy to see how two different tools both supporting say, UML, can exchange models through MOF. But what about, say, a BPMN tool exchanging information with a UML tool? This is clearly a more difficult problem. To address this problem, the modeling mavens at the OMG invented the formal concept of a 'transformation.'

A transformation is a set of rules that explains how elements in one model map to elements in model. This is not a new concept per se—after all, a GUI wizard that allows you to draw a GUI screen and then 'transforms' that 'model' into code essentially does the same thing. However, there is a big difference between a proprietary wizard that works in only one tool, and a formally specified MDA transformation, which can be read (and, as applicable, interpreted) by any other MOF-compliant tool.

So, for example, MOF can help make it possible for a group of business analysts to use a MOF-based BPMN tool to model a CIM, and then pass that information along to a MOF-based UML tool used by different group of system analysts to create a PIM. In this case, we just need a formally specified BPMN-to-UML transformation, which, conveniently, is itself also described in a special MOF-based model transformation language called Query/View/Transformation (QVT).

By the way, MOF itself defines a dynamic programmatic interface (i.e., an API) for tools to query each other and exchange model information. However, in order to better facilitate certain kinds of tool integration, MOF-based information can also be exchanged in document format via a special XML-based version of MOF called XML Metadata Interchange (XMI). This fits nicely in with environments that are already exchanging information using XML.

So, now we can imagine a brave new world of MDA in which software engineers can select tools and languages of their choice to model different view-points ("best in breed"), but keep all the resulting model artifacts in synch using MOF/XMI. No longer will they have to depend on a single vendor to cover all the bases, or spend countless hours configuring complicated tool-chains, just to exchange information.

But the really good news is—you don't have to wait! There is already a free, open-source XMI-based tool integration platform you can download today: Eclipse. Yes, that's right, XMI is the format used to exchange information in Eclipse, the increasingly popular open-source software development platform. So, if two or more tools can exchange information in Eclipse, they are already de facto based on MDA, whether they explicitly say so or not.

WHITHER MDA?

Not surprisingly, over the last couple of years, the OMG and MDA have become a lot more MOF- and XMI-centric, and a lot less UML-centric. UML is still very important, and a lot of vendors and end-users support it enthusiastically, but modeling in UML per se is now just one of many ways to apply MDA.

In fact, one important 'growth area' in the MDA world is mapping many different notational systems and architectural approaches into MOF/XMI and defining standard transformations, so that they can be integrated to work in tool chains such as those supported by the Eclipse platform. Finally getting all the modeling tools on the 'shop floor' to be able to talk to each other is a key step towards developing the kind of real 'software factory' that we discussed at the beginning of this book.

Another hot area deals with how best to apply MDA to different vertical markets. As we noted in our first chapter, as of this writing, there are already nine different MDA-related Task Forces (TFs) and Special Interest Groups (SIGs) formally operating within the OMG, including Real Time and Embedded Systems, C4I, Finance, Healthcare, Life Science Research, Manufacturing Technology and Industrial Systems, Software-Based Communications, Space, and Transportation. But these represent just the tip of a rapidly growing iceberg, as vendors and end users find new applications for MDA in every area of software engineering.

Yet another up-and-coming area of MDA has to do with what's now being called 'software process engineering.' Clearly, to use MDA, you not only need tools, but also a supporting process, which can be very useful to formalize. To this end, the OMG has developed a MDA standard called Software Process Engineering Metamodel (SPEM). At this writing, SPEM is relatively new, but it has the potential of allowing users to formally model and configure the processes by which they invoke tools and tooling chains.

DIFFERENT STROKES

So how does all this relate to our six MDA case studies? The most important point to remember as you read through these case studies is this: there is no one single way to do MDA, and there never will be. There will always be any number of valid approaches to applying MDA, depending on what you want to achieve. Just how broadly this maxim applies is amply illustrated by the case studies themselves.

But if this is so, then what makes something MDA, and what makes MDA a 'standard?' As you read our case studies, the common thread throughout all of them is that, for each step in the software lifecycle—requirements gathering, business modeling, systems architecture, application design, software development, testing, deployment, integration—there are formally defined modeling artifacts, expressed in (or mapped to) an industry standard notation/language or some close variant or extension.

Furthermore, in each case there are also well-articulated ways of moving and/or transforming the associated model elements created at each step so they can be carried forward (or in some cases backward) throughout the rest of the lifecycle process. That is, in each case, someone asked beforehand, "How can we make sure that the information we gather and the analysis we perform at each step flows properly to subsequent steps?" and "To what extent can we leverage industry modeling standards to automate this process to save time and money, reduce errors, and improve quality."

If this sounds to you remarkably like the vision of a 'software factory,' then you are definitely on the right track. But, you might ask, couldn't this be accomplished without a universal standard like MDA? In one sense, the answer is 'yes'—it is certainly possible for one vendor, or one end-user, or one project to create their own proprietary model-driven software lifecycle process and supporting tool-chain without the aid of a universal standard.

However, MDA exists today because the members of OMG—vendors, end-users, and consultants, many of whom had already tried 'rolling their own' model-driven approaches—got tired of trying to constantly reinvent the model-driven wheel. Just as in other fields, they would prefer that their tools and artifacts 'plug-and-play' with a minimum of time, cost, and effort.

Now, by following a set of standards like MDA, software organizations can design and implement their desired model-driven processes and tool-chains far faster and more efficiently than from scratch. And the really good news is that they can use MDA to achieve those results without getting boxed into a corner with a single language, product or vendor. In a nutshell, that's what MDA is all about.

FURTHER READING

The following books provide a good introduction to MDA.

Model Driven Architecture: Applying MDA to Enterprise Computing, by David S. Frankel, Wiley, 2003, ISBN: 0471319201.

MDA Distilled, by Stephen J. Mellor, Kendall Scott, Axel Uhl, and Dirk Weise, Addison-Wesley Object Technology Series (Paperback), 2004, ISBN: 0201788918.

MDA Explained: The Model Driven Architecture—Practice and Promise, by Anneke Kleppe, Jos Warmer, and Wim Bast, Addison-Wesley Professional, 2003, ISBN: 032119442X.

We also recommend the OMG's *MDA Guide Version 1.0.1*, available at *http://www.omg.org/docs/omg/03-06-01.pdf*. And for a much more extensive reading list, visit the OMG's Reading Room at *http://www.omg.org/mda/reading-room.htm*.

GLOSSARY

BPMN Business Process Modeling Notation.

BPEL Business Process Execution Language.

CASE Computer-Assisted Software Engineering.

CEO Chief Executive Officer.

CIM See *Computation-Independent Model*.

CIO Chief Information Officer.

CMM The Capability Maturity Model for software, which was developed by the Software Engineering Institute at Carnegie-Mellon University.

CMMI Capability Maturity Model Integration, which was developed by the Software Engineering Institute at Carnegie-Mellon University.

Common Information Model An implementation-independent, object-oriented schema for describing network management information, developed and maintained by the Distributed Management Task Force (*www.dmtf.org*).

Common Warehouse Metamodel (CWM) The Common Warehouse Metamodel is an OMG standard that describes metadata interchange among data warehousing, business intelligence, knowledge management, and portal technologies.

Computation-Independent Model (CIM) A Computation-Independent Model expresses the workings of a system without showing any detail of its structure or operation. A CIM is sometimes called a domain model (more specifically, a "business model") and it uses a "modeling vocabulary" that is familiar to subject matter experts in that domain.

CORBA Common Object Request Broker Architecture, an OMG standard for distributed object systems.

COTS Commercial Off-The-Shelf system.

CPIC   Capital Planning and Investment Control.

CRUD   Create, Read, Update, Delete (all of which are fundamental data storage operations).

CWM   See *Common Warehouse Metamodel*.

DoD   U.S. Department of Defense.

DSL   Domain Specific Language.

ebXML   Electronic Business XML, a standard for exchanging XML business messages over the Internet.

EDOC   The OMG's UML Profile for Enterprise Distributed Object Computing (available at *http://www.omg.org/technology/documents/formal/edoc.htm*).

EJB   Enterprise Java Beans.

FEA   Federal enterprise architecture.

General Relationship Model   ISO standard 10165-7 (available at *www.iso.org*), a standard that provides a model for reasoning about, representing, managing, and developing specifications about relationships in a way that is independent of representation mechanisms.

GOTS   Government Off-The-Shelf system.

GRM   See *General Relationship Model*.

IS   Information systems.

JMS   Java Messaging Service

LOB   Line of business.

Mark   A mark specifies a particular mapping in a model (e.g., from a model element to some aspect of its implementation on a specific technology platform).

MDA   See *model-driven architecture*.

Meta Object Facility (MOF)   The Meta Object Facility is an OMG standard that provides a common facility for managing metamodels. If two different metamodels are both MOF-conformant, models based on them can reside in the same repository and can be manipulated by MOF-conformant tools.

metamodel   A model of a model; metadata that represents the concepts within an information domain.

model   A formal specification of the structure and/or function of a system.

Model Driven Architecture   An approach to software engineering and system definition based on the creation of precise and formal models of the problem domain, the supporting computer system, and the technology implementation.

MOF   See *Meta Object Facility.*

NASA   U.S. National Aeronautics and Space Administration.

Object Management Group (OMG)   The Object Management Group is an open membership not-for-profit consortium that produces and maintains computer industry specifications for interoperable enterprise applications (see *www.omg.org*).

OMG   See *Object Management Group.*

PIM   See *Platform-Independent Model.*

Platform-Independent Model (PIM)   A Platform-Independent Model expresses the workings of a computer system to support the requirements specified in a Computation-Independent Model (CIM), but in a way that does not depend on any specific technology platform.

Platform-Specific Model (PSM)   A Platform-Specific Model combines the specifications in a Platform-Independent Model (PIM) with the details of how that system is implemented on a particular technology platform.

POC   Proof of concept.

PSM   See *Platform-Specific Model.*

Reference Model for Open Distributed Computing   ISO/IEC 10746 (available at *www.iso.org*), one of the foundational standards on which MDA is based.

RM-ODP   See *Reference Model for Open Distributed Computing.*

SDLC   Software Development Life Cycle.

SEI   The Software Engineering Institute, which is sponsored by the U.S. Department of Defense and operated by Carnegie-Mellon University.

SME   Subject matter expert.

SOA   Service-oriented architecture.

Stereotype   A UML stereotype is user-specified modeling element defined in terms of existing modeling elements.

UDDI   Universal Description Discover and Integration, a directory model for web services.

UML   See *Unified Modeling Language.*

Unified Modeling Language (UML)   An Object Management Group (OMG) standard for modeling software artifacts.

VA   U.S. Veterans Administration.

VCA   Value chain analysis.

WS   Web services.

WSDL   Web Services Definition Language.

XMI   See *XML Metadata Interchange*.

XML Metadata Interchange   XML Metadata Interchange format is an OMG standard that specifies an XML-based information interchange model, which allows the exchange of metadata in a standardized way.

XPDL   XML Process Definition Language.

XP   Microsoft's Windows XP operating system.

INDEX